KIERKEGAARD STUDIES
IN SCANDINAVIA

PUBLICATIONS OF THE KIERKEGAARD SOCIETY, COPENHAGEN

I

Methods and Results of

KIERKEGAARD STUDIES IN SCANDINAVIA

A Historical and Critical Survey

BY

AAGE HENRIKSEN

M. A.

EJNAR MUNKSGAARD

COPENHAGEN 1951

Printed in Denmark
—
Vald. Pedersens Bogtrykkeri
København

In 1944 the University of Copenhagen set as the subject for a prize paper "The History of Kierkegaard Studies in the Scandinavian Countries". For his paper on this subject Mr. Aage Henriksen was awarded the gold medal of the University. It is here published in a revised and enlarged form. The Kierkegaard Society welcomes this opportunity of making the working methods and results of Scandinavian Kierkegaard research known to the large circle of lovers of Kierkegaard who do not read the Scandinavian languages. The Society wishes to thank the Trustes of the Rask-Ørsted Foundation, who have granted financial aid for the publication, and likewise Miss Annie I. Fausbøll, M.A. who is responsible for the translation.

With this treatise the Søren Kierkegaard Society inaugurates a series of publications of interest to students of Kierkegaard all over the world.

On behalf of the Executive Committee

N. H. Søe
Professor of Theology,
University of Copenhagen
President
8, Gentoftegade, Gentofte.

F. J. Billeskov Jansen
Professor of Literature
University of Copenhagen
Vice-President
20, Frydendalsvej, Copenhagen V.

Niels Thulstrup, M.Th.
Secretary
17, Loevfroevej, Soeborg, Denmark.

CONTENTS

The number of pages given in brackets after quotations refer to the work under discussion in the particular passage, e.g. (p. 117); or to Søren Kierkegaard's work in the second edition, as e.g. (6,265), or to Søren Kierkegaard's papers, likewise in the second edition, as e.g. (II A 805), in accordance with the special arrangement of the edition, cf. p. 64.

INTRODUCTION

Viewpoints

Within the humanities the relation of parts to totalities has only exceptionally been so clearly or convincingly elucidated that an isolated study of a subject can at the outset be dismissed as valueless. The enquirer's choice of subject, his point of view, must as a rule be regarded as a private matter, which is characteristic of him as a human being more than as a scholar. It is the treatment of the subject, his manner of arguing and combining, his method, which shows his scholarly competence.

Within Kierkegaard-research it is otherwise. Since its beginning there has been disagreement concerning viewpoints as well as methods; most vehement, however, in the case of viewpoints. Søren Kierkgaard himself has most thoroughly prepared the way for this conflict, amongst other things by his book "The Point of View for my Work as an Author" which was written in 1848, but published posthumously in 1859. Here he endeavours to show that the individual works of his authorship belong together in an indivisible production, and that his personal life has been subordinate and adjusted to his work as an author in such a way that his life and work appear as a totality, a spiritual complex, whose parts and aspects must not be regarded, and cannot be interpreted, isolatedly, but only as parts of a long spun-out half human, half divine process of reflection, whose organising thought has been to point out, without authority, the Christianity of the New Testament. This attempt by Søren Kierkegaard to create unity in his life work and show the way to future interpreters has produced uncertainty and bewilderment. The disagreement as to what is the proper attitude to assume towards the Kierkegaardian complex, has gone so far that some enquirers have disputed, not only the validity of other enquirers' results, but simply the very existence of a subject concerning which a literature has already grown up. The cause of the confusion now is not only that Søren Kierkegaard's viewpoint for his activity as an author differs considerably from that which his interpreters naturally feel prompted to adopt, but also that Søren Kierkegaard's literary understanding of himself is not constant. The direct statements concerning his production which he prepared in the 1840s have indeed as their common aim that of uniting and giving perspective, but the unifying ideas change, so that the application of the later excludes the application of the earlier statements.

If, for instance, we try to understand what was Søren Kierkegaard's exact intention in using pseudonyms, we are led to a decisive ambiguity in his self-interpretation. When he began to issue his pseudonymous writings he apparently intended, or it was his intention in principle, to keep his own person entirely outside. When "Either-Or" appeared there was, in fact, for some time a doubt as to who had written it, a doubt which Søren Kierkegaard himself sought to strengthen in the article "Who is the Author of Either—Or"?, which urges the expediency of the author remaining unknown. Not until February 1846 did he admit in "First and Last Explanation", which is a supplement to "Unscientific Postscript" that he was the author of the authors and explain that the essential reason for the pseudonymous machinery was "the production itself, which for the sake of the dialogue, of the psychologically varied difference in the individualities poetically demanded that unconcern in good and evil, in contrition and elation, in despair and arrogance, in suffering and exultation etc. which is only ideally limited by the psychological consequence which no actually existing person within the moral bounds of reality dare permit himself or will want to permit himself" (7,616). And he alleges that the readers who have summarily identified him with the pseudonyms "really have cheated themselves by getting my personal identity to drag along instead of a poetically-real author's dually reflected light individuality to dance with; paralogistically intruding, have deceived themselves by meaninglessly eliciting my private individuality from the evasive dialectical duality of qualitative contrasts". (7,618).—In "The Point of View" we read, however, that the duality in his authorship was from the very outset represented by: "Either—Or" and "Two Edifying Discourses" and not, as had erroneously been supposed, by the first and second parts of "Either—Or"; that "while "Either—Or" attracted all the attention and no one heeded "Two Edifying Discourses", these nevertheless meant that it was, precisely, the edifying aspect which was to be brought to the fore, and that the author was a religious author who, therefore, had never himself written anything æsthetic, but used pseudonyms for all the æsthetic works, while the "Two Edifying Discourses" were by Magister Kierkegaard" (13,556-57);

the pseudonymity is here his incognito for the religious, the duality of the æsthetic and the religious is the sustaining principle of his authorship, and therefore the series of publications, after two years' exclusive religious production, is concluded, "as a testimony and as a precaution, with the small æsthetic article by a pseudonym: Inter et Inter" (13,558). It is thus emphasised here that the prerequisite for understanding the spirit of his production is the recognition that the contrasts are kept together in one mind. Further Kierkegaard explains in special chapters that he adapted his personal conduct so as to support the effect of the books; when his production was predominantly æsthetic he tried to create the illusion of an idler in the eyes of his readers, later when it was predominantly religious he practised Christian self-denial in all humility.

It appears from this that different functions are assigned to his pseudonymity, and that it is asserted to be carried through with varying degrees of effect. It has two forms, each corresponding to a particular kind of religious tactics; and to make the confusion complete, Kierkegaard calls both kinds indirect communication. In his production up to and including "Unscientific Postscript" indirect communication is contrasted with Hegelian direct communication of objective knowledge, the method being that the narrator, after producing his testimony, destroys himself and leaves the reader deserted with a statement in which qualitative contrasts clash. The reader can only save himself from the dilemma by a personal recognition and solution of the problems. In "The Point of View" the indirect statement is contrasted with the direct preaching, which would lead the hearer to the truth by persuasion. It is interpreted as a method of inveigling him into the truth, by the teacher's pretending to be in the pupil's situation (delusion) and thus achieving personal contact; thereafter he slowly uncovers the truth, so that the learner, absorbed in his interest, with the speed of abandonment, is made to run right into the most decisive precepts of the religion. Hence, in the first case salvation is to come by self-activity, in the second case by imitation, by the current in the works being induced in the reader. In the first instance the pseudonymity is to be taken absolutely, in the second instance as a provisional screen suggesting the author's feeling of estrangement among the æsthetic categories. That one of the very few writings of Søren Kierkegaard which no one attributed to him before he admitted the authorship himself, belongs to the last group, where the unity behind the contrasts was to be divined, is another matter which tells us a good deal of how the "Point of View" came into existence. It was "The Crisis and a Crisis in the Life of an

Actress", the short series of articles from 1848, which was to show that the duality of the æsthetic and the religious was present to the very last; he himself called it pseudonymous, but it was actually anonymous, signed with the mark: Inter et Inter, which presumably can never, or at any rate not in Kierkegaard's sense, be called a pseudonym, that is to say, a poetically real author-individuality.

From this schematic explanation of an ambiguity in his self-interpretations it will be understood that we cannot quite simply adopt Søren Kierkegaard's view of Søren Kierkegaard's production. The opposite procedure of disregarding Søren Kierkegaard's explanations about the importance of the indirect statement for the construction of his work and about the purpose and consequence of the pseudonymity will, however, also entail difficulties and unsatisfactory solutions. Torsten Bohlin, for instance, in his investigation of Søren Kierkegaard's dogmatic views arrives at the result that Kierkegaard, in the books "Philosophical Fragments" and "The Concept of Dread" published with four days' interval, gives two irreconcilable determinations of the concept of sin. It is a matter of surprise to him, an interesting psychological problem that Kierkegaard was able to avoid noticing the contradiction between the two works and the inconsistency in his own thinking. It is undeniable that there is a similarity between Torsten Bohlin pondering on the interesting psychological problem and the contemporary readers of Søren Kierkegaard who "unfamiliar with the courtesies of a distancing ideality, by a mistaken intrusion on my actual personality have garbled their impression of the pseudonymous books, have cheated themselves, really have cheated themselves by getting my personal reality to drag along instead of a poetically real author's dually reflected light ideality to dance with— — —" (7,618). But if then we follow the author's suggestion "to cite the respective pseudonymous author's name, not mine", then indeed the special problem is solved, but it returns as the problem of the entire production.

It will appear from these examples that whether or not we follow Søren Kierkegaard's directions, we shall have reason to regret both procedures. This is a conclusion drawn on the basis of few observations but which will be confirmed by the succeeding analysis of the main works written about Kierkegaard. A point of view which neither violates the totality nor the separate parts does not seem to have been attained by anybody. The core of the authorship has not been penetrated.

Of the many viewpoints adopted in the course of time three stand out as simple and primary, the remainder being derivatives and combinations of them. The three main points of view group themselves in two pairs of contrasts: opposed to the contention that the study of Søren Kierkegaard should aim at understanding the expression, the literary form, stands the view that the contents of the production, the thoughts and ideas, are the central thing. The group of enquirers who study the contents divide into two formations, one of which maintains that the individual works should be understood as parts of the totality of the production, the other, that it is the history of Søren Kierkegaard's spiritual development which unites the production.

There is no consistent adherence to the formal point of view in Scandinavian research. It has been adopted in Germany by a dialectic school under the direction of the ingenious theologian Hermann Diem. In a treatise entitled "Methode der Kierkegaard Forschung" (the Method of Kierkegaard Research) (Zwischen den Zeiten 1928, p. 140 seq.) he sharply maintains the impossibility of arriving at any understanding whatever of Søren Kierkegaard's life work by means of the current comparative and genetic methods. Kirkegaard was an existential dialectician, declares Diem in good agreement with certain statements by Kierkegaard himself; but he had no system, only a method, the dually conceived dialectical method—behind which, it is true, there were certain views. Its application requires two persons, teacher and pupil, in Socratic conversation with each other, the one who has knowledge asking the questions, the one who seeks knowledge giving the answers. When both have their attention directed towards the same subject during the conversation, it is the questioner's mission to release his counterpart from his immediate relation to the subject—which may be philosophy, or the prejudice that man is capable of knowing anything at all—by resolving it into nothing by abstraction. If they succeed in bringing this course to a close, a new inner process, self-activity, will thereby be released in the questioned person. He must now, personally, without the assistance of teacher or knowledge, solve the problems of his existence. It was in order to arrive at this result: that the person questioned, the reader, should be released from all external authorities and learn to think for himself, that Søren Kierkegaard, adopting a pseudonym, attempted to disappear behind his works in Socratic concealment. The work done to demonstrate the personal element in his production is therefore in conflict with Søren Kierkegaard's express wishes and an obstacle to the right understanding of his work. Comparative studies of his teaching and that of the Church, of his and Hegel's doctrines, are likewise at best useless, because Søren Kierkegaard had no doctrine, merely a method. We gain no understanding of or profit from Kierkegaard's books by talking of him, but by entering into conversation with him.

Just as Diem can prove the justice of his opinion by quoting Søren Kierkegaard, notably "Unscientific Postscript", so also representatives of the view that Kierkegaard's production forms a totality can refer to his self-interpretations, not only to the "Point of View" but to later publications such as "Of my Authorship" and the preface to "Two Discourses at the Communion on Fridays" from 1851. Rudin has done so and thus taken the concept "totality" in a narrower sense, i.e. he has accepted Søren Kierkegaard's contention that his production, with the aid of Providence, has been built up around the one constructive idea of calling attention without authority to the Christianity of the New Testament. The totality view in a wider sense, energetically maintained by Emanuel Hirsch and Valter Lindström among others, covers the conception that the course of the production may have been determined by Kierkegaard's personal history, but it is sustained and pervaded by a religious totality view; this totality view, which can be deduced from the works and described systematically, is the unity behind the multitudinous and varied production, against the background of which apparent inconsistencies in Kierkegaard's thinking, and contradictions between the individual publications, resolve themselves into a harmony.

The third point of view, that which has dominated Scandinavian research and according to which the individual works must be interpreted separately and their peculiarity be explained psychologically, can be scientifically defended by a well-founded distrust of Søren Kierkegaard's retrospective interpretations and the substantiated observation of changes in his views; this is indeed the reason why several theologians, among them Torsten Bohlin, have joined in the psychological study of Søren Kierkegaard. The majority of enquirers, however, have been so strongly and irresistibly drawn towards the obscure and intriguing connection between Kierkegaard's private history and his public works, which already his contemporaries could dimly see, that no argument against a purely personal historical and genetic explanation of his production has been able to deter them from adopting the psychological view.

Periods

It is an old-established view that the "actual" study of Søren Kierkegaard was started with Georg Brandes' book about him in 1877. The notion is based on the fact that it was this book that first described the approximate course of Søren Kierkegaard's life and raised the greater part of those problems around which Danish research has later centred with such great patience. The book forms the starting-point of a tradition; it contains the earliest contributions to the solution of the Kierkegaardian enigmas that still count.

Against the background of the literature on Søren Kierkegaard available about the middle of the 1870s, it is, however, another, less tangible, and now also for good reasons less conspicuous, feature of Brandes' book which separates it decisively from its predecessors, namely its striving for objectivity. Brandes is the first to show the will and the power to understand the Kierkegaardian, and the first to divide his energy equally between understanding and judging. No one was willing to acknowledge this at the time the book was published; and in recent years, owing to the very considerable residue of the author's convictions which despite all progress has been preserved in it, it has rightly been grouped among Brandes' semi-agitatorial writings, so that the fact has been slurred over. For that very reason it informs us of another of the variable quantities that distinguish Kierkegaardian research.

To a small group of revolutionary spirits, such as Luther and Karl Marx, it applies that the literature about them has only late, and in part not at all, assumed a dispassionate scientific-historical character; the atmosphere surrounding them is still so much alive that it can be sensed. Hostility or open admiration are still attitudes with which we must reckon as the covert or overt sources of inspiration for works dealing with them. The same applies to Søren Kierkegaard on a smaller scale. About him too there is something physically present, rendering possible an intimate reaction. Neither the passionate and penetrative spirit of his production, or the shocking and mystifying aspect of his personal existence, nor what was wounding and goading in his final unscrupulous behaviour, will fully explain the force of attraction issuing from him; they are aspects of his highly diversified existence which closed in around the unrevealed core of his personality. He has been called the ant-lion in Danish intellectual life. In a way somewhat different from what he wished he has retained the faculty of making his readers react subjectively.

If we disregard the suddenly enhanced interest in Kierkegaard of the very last few years, which will probably one day find its own explanation, three stages can be distinguished in the Scandinavian process of habituation to the Søren Kierkegaard phenomenon; first a period extending from the beginning of the conflict with the Church in 1854 to about 1870, in which the literature about him consists in polemics—in part very violent. Then, in the last 30 years of the century a period in which research and conviction are so equally conjoined that as a whole it may be characterised as semi-agitatorial. And finally the period from the turn of the century to our own time, which may with some reserve be termed sober.

What happens in the course of this period of just under a hundred years is a gradual liberation from the impression of Søren Kierkegaard's concluding attack on the Church and Clergy, which renders possible a gradual extension of the surface of contact between him and his readers. Their angle of vision was extended in 1877 by Brandes' book; from comprising the onslaught in 1854-55 it now took in the whole Søren Kierkegaard. And some time after the turn of the century, a differentiation began to appear, the introduction of the many special viewpoints. Prior to these leaps in the development of Søren Kierkegaard research we have on both occasions the publication of the first volumes of an edition of Kierkegaard's posthumous papers, namely Barfod and Gottsched's edition in 8 volumes in 1869-81, and Heiberg and Kuhr's edition in 20 volumes in 1909-49.

The coincidence is not accidental. An exposition of the inward coherence of Søren Kierkegaard's history could not be written until an essential part of his papers had appeared in print, and a comprehensive specialised study of biographical and literary details could not be undertaken until they were available in a complete and critical edition. The dependence of a study on the material is self-evident; but the immediate change in the form of study of Søren Kierkegaard as soon as these conditions were present, shows that the background both of the editions and the studies was the same scientific historical situation. If, therefore, we are to delimit more precisely the two periods in which the occupation with Kierkegaard has the character of research, it will be natural to fix as the initial years the time when the first two volumes of the two editions of the papers were published. The two periods of the present exposition then chance to be of exactly the same length, namely from 1869 to 1909 and from 1909 to 1949.

Plan and Method

The exposition that follows of the history of Søren Kierkegaard research comprises the so-called "actual" research and disregards the theological polemics. The main division of the material is chronological: each of the two periods fills a part. My exposition of the works of the period begins with an account of the respective edition of Kierkegaard's papers, and terminates with a survey of the period. The intermediate chapters discuss the books on Søren Kierkegaard, placed according to their viewpoint, but not those described above. Only in exceptional cases could the attitude assumed towards the special Kierkegaardian problems be used as a basis of disposition, because it has played a role which, though decisive, has not been sufficiently recognised in the history of Kierkegaard research. For, very often the necessary connection between viewpoints and particular interpretation-problems has not been clear to the enquirers, so that these, as for instance Eduard Geismar, have overcome the difficulties by a temporary change of viewpoint, without therefore accepting the consequences of the new point of view. In the main part of the treatise, Part 2, the viewpoints are of an external, purely systematic kind, as will appear from the table of contents. In Part 1, which comprises subjectively marked comprehensive expositions, the authors have been grouped more as poets according to their personal or literary type.—In the individual chapters the enquirers are discussed in chronological order in so far as a displacement would not contribute to simplify the exposition.

Finally it must be said about the critical method of my work that it consists in giving, to the best of my ability, a full and loyal account, so formed that the enquirer's own method, his way of combining, will appear from it; how the works link up should appear in the reproduction. After an account of a production inaugurating a tradition an attempt is made to describe the method and demonstrate its flaws, if any, first in general, and then with examples of the practical consequences of the methodological defects. This mode of procedure should have at least two advantages, namely, that the exposition will assume its own form and not be hopelessly flooded with discussions of details and records of the varying enquirers' opinions of the same matter, and that it does not presuppose that the writer is in possession of the correct answer to the numerous questions raised by enquirers in the course of time. But he will not of course be able entirely to avoid some criticism on the basis of his opinion of the Kierkegaardian, any more than it can be avoided that the special qualifications of the critic will leave their traces in his work. In the present case this means that the writer is more familiar with literary history than with theological and psychiatric concepts.

Section I

RESEARCH FROM 1869 TO 1909

1. The First Edition of the "Papers"

The first edition of Kierkegaard's posthumous papers, "Søren Kierkegaard. Efterladte Papirer", consists of 9 volumes which appeared in 8 instalments: 1-2 (1833-38, 1839-43) in 1869; 3 (1844-46) in 1872; 4 (1847) in 1877; 5, 6, and 7 (1848, 49 and 50) all in 1880; and 8 and 9 (1851-53, 1854-55) both in 1881. The first four volumes were edited by H. P. Barfod (1834-1892), a former newspaper editor, who in 1865 was employed by P. C. Kierkegaard as amanuensis at the episcopal office in Aalborg; when Barfod in 1877 had to stop his activity "owing to the circumstances" (probably circumstances connected with P. C. Kierkegaard's resignation of his office and increasing fear of having assumed undue rights over his brother's literary remains), the work was undertaken by H. Gottsched (1849-?), a German theologian, master in a secondary school. This happened in 1879 and in the course of few years the five remaining volumes were issued. With its c. 4000 pages the edition now contains well over half as many typographical units as the new 20-volume edition.

Barfod has not acquired the best of reputations as editor; both his contemporaries and his successors have raised serious objections to his work. He was indeed a confused thinker and made several irremediable mistakes of a diplomatic and archival kind. Hence there has been a tendency to overlook his merits, which were not few. Not only did he undertake a task which for years had gone abegging among Kierkegaard's acquaintances, and for 14-15 years devoted much of his time and his initiative to it, but during the work he also proved himself possessed of a feeling for Kierkegaard's greatness, even in its more bizarre expressions, a feeling which was foreign to most of his contemporaries, and a sure sense of the psychological perspective in aphorisms and associations and in Kierkegaard's own corrections, trifles of which no one else was then able to appraise the value.

Within the limits set by his fundamental confusion, he was a man of intellect, not without gifts.

The great unwillingness to give Barfod his due is probably for the most part caused by the heinous carelessness with which he treated Kierkegaard's manuscripts. With ill-suppressed passion it is explained in the preface to Heiberg and Kuhr's edition of the papers that "when the manuscript remains in the year 1875 were handed over to the Library, the oldest part of them had, up to the year 1847, been treated with a roughness that was fatal to their completeness and whole state of preservation. In the autumn of 1867 H. P. Barfod was given "a free hand with regard to the literary remains of Søren Kierkegaard", in order to make "preparation for their eventual publication". During continually varying views of the arrangement and editorship, the oldest part of the manuscripts was by cutting, pasting up, signing, filling with written instructions for the compositor and much else, overscoring, and correcting throughout etc. prepared to be sent to press in part as manuscript for Barfod's edition of the "Posthumous Papers"——. (I, p. IX). We receive an impression of the extent of the ravages when the new editors inform us that for 21 p.c. of the items in their first volume and for 11 p.c. of the items in their second volume they have been obliged to use Barfod's edition as their source. And we can form a conception of what invaluable matter the maculation may have destroyed when it is pointed out as particularly deplorable that of the notes II A 220-29 from the year 1838 six are only represented by index-words from Barfod's list; among the three preserved we find the exceedingly significant: "There is an indescribable joy— —" (19/5), which is normally regarded by enquirers as evidence of a religious change in Søren Kierkegaard. The loss of intellectual milieu is bitter here more than in any other place. What may further, apart from demonstrable destruction, have been lost of details in the texts which are only known from Barfod's transmission, appears from the notes of which the original manuscripts have been preserved. There is hardly one in which Barfod has not made small stylistic and orthographical corrections, and there are several in which words have been misread and sentences omitted. As an example of a very much damaged entry may be mentioned II A 68: "To-day again the same scene—I managed to get out to Rørdam, however —good Heavens, why was this inclination to awake just at this moment— O how I feel I am alone—O cursed be that arrogant satisfaction of standing alone—All will now despise me—O but Thou, my God, do not desert me—let me live and mend my ways—". Barfod's version of the same entry is as follows: "To-day again the same scene—I managed, however, to get out to . . .—Heavens, why was this inclination to awake just at this moment. O, how I feel that *I am alone*—O, the curse of that arrogant satisfaction at standing alone—Thou, my God, do not desert me." (1, p. 123).

It is only natural that the entirely unnecessary material neglect of the papers should have influenced posterity's judgment of Barfod's edition; but at the same time there has been a tendency to estimate it according to the requirements of a later period's representatives of psychological microscopy; and there is something unjust in this, for the increasing needs of Kierkegaard students are due, precisely, to the growth of understanding to which Barfod's edition decidedly contributed. For a diplomatic edition in a philological sense the time about 1870 was not ripe.

It is by the arrangement and selection of the papers that Barfod's edition may justly be evaluated. Both these aspects of the preparation for press are naturally marked by the total plan of the edition. This was "to give a collection of materials; as far as possible, ordered archives of loose, often not even mutually connected, *documentary evidence* for (the use of) the future account of Søren Kierkegaard's history". (I, p. XI). It was a large and exhaustive biography which Barfod pictured to himself; for its author he would supply the material. For the pedantic analyses and subtle descriptions of the slow structural changes of reflection-complexes he had, for very good reasons, no thought.

With regard to the arrangement of the material, its determination as biographical material meant that the chronological view came to dominate over the systematic. The reproduction of diaries such as the JJ diary or the first of the 36 NB diaries thus took place in fragments, and letters, loose slips, and unprinted polemical articles are inserted in their chronological place in the text. Thus, for instance, in the third volume the diary is interrupted after an entry dated 10.6.1845, and an unposted letter, connected with Copenhagen news of the following week, but otherwise unconnected with the diary, is inserted. But the chronological principle could not be consistently adhered to without loss of grasp and dramatic tension. From and including the third volume (2nd instalment) we therefore see Barfod collecting available material under headings from the imagined biography, e.g. Polemics against Heiberg, the Corsair and Goldschmidt. Thus the chronological arrangement is combined with an arrangement according to subjects in those cases where Søren Kierkegaard's life-history contains novel-like chapters.

The plan of giving the texts in an essentially chronological order entails another difficulty, the dating of the entries. In the main Barfod ignored this problem by chiefly selecting entries of a personal nature for his edition, and their relative chronology can as a rule be determined with a fair degree of accuracy by their placing. In cases where he had no elementary criteria of dating to go by but had to establish the date of entry by the train of thought revealed in the texts and by their literary and historical allusions, he occasionally shows an astonishing uncertainty. This applies especially to the earliest entries. Thus Barfod opens the first volume with some presumably fictitious letters criticising the times, the composition of which he assigns to 1835. The new editors date the same entries (I, A 328-41) at 1836-37, which may be substantiated among other things by several allusions to Martensen's lectures and writings in those years.

As regards the selection of texts there were several points to be considered, partly the volume and literary quality of the books, partly the feelings of the contemporaries of Kierkegaard to whom reference was made in the papers. In the qualitative reduction of the material the guiding principle was that what could actually be expected to be of interest was the diaries of the Søren Kierkegaard known to the public. "Since, however, the importance and treatment of the material gradually increase as we proceed through the series of the above-mentioned thirty-six "Diaries" (March 1846-the spring of 1855), there will probably, when this part of the papers is one day submitted to the public, be a much greater interest in the contents of these diaries proper than that which may immediately be expected to be taken in this introductory first volume.— — — Entirely to skip some or all of these years (1833-43) so as to let the public at once draw upon the source of the more coherent entries, would hardly do, however, if the whole work were not to be without its antecedents, the building without its portal." (P.P. I, p. XI). The elimination then especially came to concern entries relating to studies, drafts for and variants of the works proper, that is to say, texts which in the new edition are grouped under sections B and C, and notes and sketches from Kierkegaard's first years of study.

Curtailments and omissions for diplomatic reasons were only made in scant measure by Barfod. His texts have merely a minimum of the square brackets filled with dots which indicate editorial intervention. Apart from P. C. Kierkegaard, none of Søren Kierkegaard's acquaintances were spared either from very intimate comments or very trenchant attacks. The worst of them were directed against Regine, Goldschmidt, Grundtvig, and Rasmus

Nielsen. Barfod's frankness in this respect was characterised as ruffianly by contemporary reviewers. This judgment was unjust in so far as the majority of critics did not absolutely assert that the papers were published at the wrong time. One could hardly have raised any objection to such a view. The edition did in fact appear a score of years too early if offence to the survivors was to have been avoided. But if it were to be published it could hardly be different. A text leaving out polemics and confessions would in the main be without value. And a text including this material, but edited ad usum Delphini, would give a decidedly distorted picture of Søren Kierkegaard. On this point Barfod defended himself against his critics in the preface to the third volume, with reference to Regine in the following polite and elegant turns of phrase: "I am said to have been guilty of great indiscretion in reprinting in the "Posthumous Papers" what was concerned with Søren Kierkegaard's youthful love. Since these painful outbursts of deep feeling all raised the woman to whom they were directed to the throne of admiration and excellence I did not suppose that now, after so many years, they could wound anybody; on the contrary, I was convinced that in the right place they must excite a certain pride and joy, though mixed with sadness." (P.P. II, p. XIII). And with regard to Goldschmidt, and thus also to Søren Kierkegaard's literary and religious opponents in general, Barfod puts forward the following weighty arguments: "Now to let these pronouncements of Søren Kierkegaard's pass quite unnoticed and unused when the remains were otherwise to be published seemed to me an impossibility, an untruth. Nevertheless, at times, especially before I reached this volume, I conceived the possibility of having to lay this section aside for the time being—I arrived at the result, however, that the "Corsair's" conduct towards Kierkegaard belonged to literary history, that it was only fair now to let Søren Kierkegaard speak more fully in a matter which had so deeply and bitterly stirred his heart and to which he had already referred in some pages of "The Point of View". The situation is besides far easier for Mr. Goldschmidt's literary reputation when he is himself alive at the publication of the papers than if they had not appeared until after his death.—A characteristic of Kierkegaard's polemic was its frank unscrupulousness; I could not therefore see any obstacle to the publication in the unscrupulousness with which Kierkegaard wielded his weapon. Since I have further, as far as possible, let Mr. Goldschmidt speak for himself, having cited at some length the articles by him to which reference or reply was made, it seems to me that I have endeavoured to be as impartial as the circumstances permitted,—

even though I dare not hope that Mr. Goldschmidt in every part of these pages can trace the "ideal sensations" through Kierkegaard's "passionate bitterness", of which he himself has once given evidence" (P.P. II, p XII).

In the above-quoted passage, Barfod alludes to the notes and comments which he has included in the edition. They comprise quotations from the periodicals "The Corsair" and "North and South". Similar quotations from and references to old material from periodicals and newspapers Barfod has, where he deemed it necessary, largely incorporated in his text, which greatly facilitates the reading and gives the books life. In addition to this extra work in the archives Barfod applied to a number of Kierkegaard's schoolfellows and later acquaintances and asked them to tell him any matters great or small that they remembered of the deceased author. In this way he procured for the Søren Kierkegaard archives several valuable letters on which his notes in the first volume of the edition are based. They form an important corrective and supplement to Kierkegaard's own scant memories from his childhood and have furnished the main part of the anecdotal matter from which our image of Søren Kierkegaard in his first youth is formed. Among the enterprising Barfod's many ideas the recovery of this important psychological material is the only thing which later enquirers have been ready to appreciate.

The other editor, H. Gottsched, has not left any reputation of mark. When mentioned, he is praised at the expense of Barfod. He has not spoilt anything nor supplied new sources. It has merely been necessary to do his work over again.

Gottsched's redaction of the papers begins in the middle of the fourth NB diary, and the remaining 32 NB diaries are the chief manuscripts on which the five volumes of the edition which he prepared are based. He gave the texts, connected up and in chronological order, without any comments. Each volume contains a main text consisting of diaries, and a supplement consisting of unfinished or unpublished minor works: polemical articles, prefaces and the like.

His curtailment of the text was at first extremely cautious. In contrast with Barfod who, we must remember, worked with the more chaotic material from Kierkegaard's youth, Gottsched in the first volumes left out only a very few entries on account of their quality. In diplomacy, on the other hand, he went farther. He changed "nonsense-parsons" to "...-parsons" and "rump" to "R...". He left out entries relating to Kierkegaard's brother Peter and to Regine and her people, or made them partly unintelligible by inserting dots in such a way that we get an inkling of unmentionable perfidy where the manuscript has a blunt or personal expression. This tendency to take the edge off Søren Kierkegaard which can be observed sporadically in Gottsched's first volume, increased as the edition proceeded. Presumably compelled by the publisher, Gottsched in each new volume omitted an increasing number of articles, chiefly such as might give offence, or he curtailed the entries so that they only approximately reproduced Kierkegaard's thoughts. This tendency is particularly marked in the last two volumes. While Gottsched's first three volumes reproduce 85-90 p.c. of all Kierkegaard's diary entries, entire or curtailed, the last two volumes contain only about 50 p. c. of the articles in the new edition. He himself called attention to his changed course in a short preface to the 8th volume: "The text may seem somewhat more curtailed here than in the previous volumes; I think, however, that all essential matter has been included, while actual repetitions have, I think, been avoided." That it is the repetition, or rather the resumption, of old thoughts which has especially been avoided by curtailment is in so far correct. Only, it must be added that it is most frequently the daring and psychologically striking redaction that has been eliminated. Thus it can be shown that an attempt has been made to slur over the daring mood in which Søren Kierkegaard lived the last years of his life. Detailed evidence of Kierkegaard's periodical, pathological over-estimation of himself, his reflections on a possible martyrdom, and as to whether he differed from an apostle, have been almost systematically suppressed.

Summing up we may say, then, that Barfod's volumes with all their defects have been edited with resourcefulness and that they were well suited for their original purpose, while it is difficult to see for what purpose Gottsched's volumes are suited; but that our knowledge of Søren Kierkegaard would probably in spite of all have been fuller if the timid and slightly prim Gottsched who had a modern text editor's understanding of the value of manuscripts, had superintended the redaction of the collected edition.

2. G. Brandes, H. Høffding, and H. Vodskov

The first to use Søren Kierkegaard's papers methodically was Georg Brandes (1842-1927), the eminent Danish critic of Jewish descent who in the last third of the 19th century was a prominent figure in Scandinavian cultural life. From the time when, immediately after his return from an educational tour in Europe in 1871, he opened his attack on the narrow late romantic culture of Denmark until towards the close of the 1880s he grew tired of his own programme he was the central figure in the public debate, hated and admired. His ideas were those of liberalism, his medium of communication chiefly literary-historical treatises which occasionally necessitated a certain arranging of the facts. By virtue of his provocative and inspiring personality his activities became more epoch-making than his views merited. Through him a number of young writers became aware of their modernism, and by him a number of middle-aged liberals were driven back into conservatism. Hence he was unpopular in ecclesiastical circles who had so far been the custodians of Søren Kierkegaard's reputation, when in 1877 he published his book "Søren Kierkegaard. En kritisk Fremstilling i Grundrids" (SK. A critical exposition in outline.)

The book fell weightily on the minds of his contemporaries and the later literature on Søren Kierkegaard spreads in circles from it. It is with this as with the whole activity of Brandes, its value as an incitement can hardly be over-rated, whereas its scientific quality is disputable—and has been disputed.

Already by its motto Brandes' book differs from those of the other Kierkegaard enquirers; while they tune up in words which do honour to their sincerity and earnestness, Brandes quotes this more recondite sentence from Hamann as a motto for his book: "Was Tarquinius Superbus in seinem Garten mit dem Mohnköpfen sprach, verstand der Sohn, aber nicht der Bote". Interpreted in the light of the story it means that the action which all may see is a disguised message adressed to a single person only; applied to Brandes' book it probably meant that the critical exposition of Søren Kierkegaard's life and works intended for the reading public in general had another intention which it would only be granted to a few to understand. There is reason to believe that Brandes disclosed the secret himself when in 1888 he wrote to Nietzsche that his aim in writing the treatise on Søren Kierkegaard was to free the Danish people from his influence. A closer scrutiny of the book will at any rate show that in its inmost structure it has traces of a tendency which, far from being emphasised, is on the contrary concealed by the scattered attacks in a positivist spirit that Brandes takes occasion to put forward in his explanation of several of Kierkegaard's particularly reactionary views.

The 28 chapters of the book fall into four large groups: 1-9 (his disposition and upbringing), 10-15 (his betrothal and pseudonymous writings), 16-22 (his stages), 23-28 (the Corsair feud and his religious writings), which will be designated A, B, C, and D. In the 6th chapter Søren Kierkegaard's fundamental passions are determined as reverence and contempt. By way of introduction there is reason to pause at this formula which is stated by Brandes to be the key to Kierkegaard's works, and which at any rate is well suited to be the starting point for his own book. Reverence and contempt do not define character but relations; they do not characterise Søren Kierkegaard as an isolated spiritual organisation, but denote derived expressions of his qualities, reflexes in his mind arising from his meeting with the world arround him. Reverence leads him away from his ego in sincere devotion, but in his contempt there is a double current: a cold one directed against the outside world, and a warm one flowing towards his own person. Brandes himself realised perfectly that the words reverence and contempt merely covered reactions to the outside world, he closes his description of Søren Kierkegaard's original disposition and early upbringing as follows: "True dignity has neither that humility nor this comparing pride (22). Humility (22), the spirit of subjection and obsequiousness (19), a tendency to deference (23), are the primary expressions of the quality which in life is displayed as faith in authority, reverence,—correspondingly pride (22), arrogance (21), independence (109), self-satisfaction (22) manifest themselves in contempt. But how reconcile such antagonistic tendencies in a mind, tendencies that lead in the two opposite directions of self-effacement and self-assertion? In section A Brandes explains that it could be done by a corresponding cleavage of life—"before the Christian tradition and its ecclesiastical and poetical apostles he prostrated himself, before those who were outside it in their literary and political activities he had only the deadliest scorn. In his reverence he waived part of his legimate critical rights. To make up for it he claimed a place apart from the ordinary run of men in other respects" (33). That Brandes did not himself believe in this constructive solution of the problem, appears from his inserted remark that Søren Kierkegaard would probably have risen in revolt against his teachers even if they had been orthodox. Of the two basic impulses his contempt, his polemical tendency, thus probably had a certain psychological priority, even though it did not find much expression in his boyhood and youth, when Søren's natural intellectual growth was checked by his father's ponderous, hypnotic personality. In the next section, B, the obscurity in the relation between reverence and contempt, or tradition and individualism, by which Brandes himself in the first section pretended to be blinded, is transferred to Søren Kierkegaard; he discovers the category of "the single individual", but thinks it is one with the Christian tradition. His mind is balanced, the fields of activity for his passions have been staked out: his reverence is devoted to the past and its few surviving representatives, his contempt is aimed at his own time; but the clarity is merely apparent, its source is a confusion of ideas; Brandes foreshadows great earthquakes. In C the reader is allowed to rest in some retrospective chapters where the three stages of life of the pseudonyms are analysed and assessed from a radical, modernistic angle; here Brandes sets forth his views. In D the decisive collapse takes place, the break with the church and the clergy and the primate of the clergy, Bishop Mynster, previously the subject of Søren Kierkegaard's most profound veneration. His contempt had spread and eaten away large parts of the domain of his reverence. An unlimited individualism was the result: "Like other reformers hounded to death, he at last saw the misjudged rights of his personality as the only thing in the world. Even when he appealed to the scriptures he really appealed to his own interpretation of them, to himself. Just as absolutism had asserted "The state, that is I", so also he now thought, "the truth, that is I" (p. 268). And yet, in spite of all, the tension was not entirely done away with, his self-assertion was not yet absolute; Søren Kierkegaard still recognised the New Testament as his authority, and thus he died, and died an untimely death, Brandes maintains; "merely the circumstance that he continued to live would have compelled him to utter new radical and increasingly true thoughts" (p. 267). Søren Kierkegaard's contempt must finally have been directed against the Holy Scriptures themselves, and released from all the bonds of reverence he would at last have reached the point from which freedom beckons.

This movement, which is the very nerve of the book, does not merely contain Brandes' acute interpretation of Søren Kierkegaard's development but is in itself an ingenious defence of the pagan humanism of which Brandes was the advocate: it is the story of a genius who is brought up in the strictest way to protect the church and the Christian moral doctrines, but who ends by combating what he was intended to serve and is just on the point of divesting himself of the last prejudice when death tragically interrupts his work.

The spiritual process of development here described falls into three fairly sharply divided stages, which are each of them in a crucial way associated with an impression from real life. By his melancholy pietistic father, whose stooping aged figure Brandes has drawn with more genius than sympathy, Søren Kierkegaard was forced to subjection and Christian humility, but the painful crisis of the story of his betrothal harrowed his soul and gave rise to his pseudonymous production whose theory of knowledge ends in the paradox, and the categorical imperative of which is: become a "single individual". And the Corsair feud with its accompanying prolonged persecution drove the intellectual side of Christianity into the background in Søren Kierkegaard's mind. Paradox gave place to passion. From now onward it was martyrdom to be a Christian. In two great bounds Søren Kierkegaard had developed from a lacquey to a martyr.

The aim Brandes had set himself in his book about Søren Kierkegaard was to give an account of the genesis of his production. He intended to review his works, in their coherence and chronological order—so as to place them, not in literary or ecclesiastical history, but in the story of his life, and to show that each work or group of works reflected a stage in his development. But it was in the first place from his works that Kierkegaard's spiritual development was known; hence his task must be to demonstrate that precisely as it manifested itself there it was the logical outcome of the meeting between Kierkegaard's innate disposition and reality.—The above account of the plan of Brandes' book shows how he carried out his project, and it is in the execution of it that we encounter the methodical problems, not in the assertion that Kierkegaard's production, as well as that of any other writer, can be interpreted as the result of a co-operation between his psychic organisation and his experience, which I suppose but few would dispute. The difficulties were two; first, for the sake of clarity, Søren Kierkegaard's tremendously complicated psychic mechanism was to be reduced to a quantity that could be handled conveniently, and out of the mass of his experiences the few were to be selected which must be supposed to have dominated the history of his life. Further it was necessary, in spite of this simplification, to preserve the balance between the internal and external factors so that the final picture gave as true a representation of reality as a conventionalised drawing which reproduces the proportions of its theme and merely lacks its multiplicity of detail. It will hardly be possible to maintain that Brandes' solution of the problem was satisfactory.

He was most successful in his reduction of all Kierkegaard's experiences to some few, the effects of which may be regarded as particularly fatal. Here his principle of simplication joined forces with Kierkegaard's peculiar nature, which simply excluded him from a multiplicity of experiences by drawing him out of life as soon as it had stung him to the quick. Later Kierkegaard research has had nothing to alter in, though indeed something to add to, Brandes' conception of the history of the engagement and the Corsair feud as marking a turning point in Kierkegaard's life.—Less successful, on the other hand, was his attempt to define the form in which Søren Kierkegaard's mind expressed itself. I have previously dealt with the contents, and shall now examine how the formula came into being by which Brandes thought that he could characterise Kierkegaard's nature. Its basic impulses were stated to be reverence and contempt, which were also called fundamental passions. Brandes purposely avoided the expression dominant quality, because he did not wish to recall the well known category from Taine's æsthetics. In his thesis for the doctorate Brandes had vigorously disputed the doctrine of the dominant quality, nor can it be said, as has been done, that his method in the treatise on Søren Kierkegaard shows any modification of this opinion. When Taine desired to arrive at an understanding of an author's personality he tried to penetrate through the multiplicity to the moving spirit behind his genius, to that unity which he held was present in every great mind and which determined and shaped all the activities of the talented. But Brandes does not seek the core of Søren Kierkegaard's nature, but its circumscribing orbit, and that, he thought, was formed of reverence and contempt, "When he left behind him his early youth (S.K. was) endowed with all the qualities of which the character is formed, and these can be traced back to two basic impulses: etc." (p. 32). The dissociation from Taine implied in the passage just quoted corresponds precisely to the following critical remark from the thesis, "Even though we shall always, which I do not doubt, be able by segregation to find something, though often rather abstract, which is common to all the different provinces of a mind, we are unable to show how the faculty for one thing evokes the faculty for another" (XIV, p. 656, popular edition 1900). On this point Brandes' independence of Taine is thus clear; his contention—put forward in 1871, repeated in 1877—that a bedrock disposition may be shown to exist in an author's mind which, independently of what he may otherwise possess of qualities, manifests itself in all his activities, is not sensational but, on the other hand, should have the advantage of not being based on metaphysics, but on experience.

Nor was Brandes unaware of the fact that a knowledge of this bedrock disposition cannot be gained by means of an exact scientific and indisputable method. That criticism is an art was one of the maxims he tried to establish in his thesis. The formula for the circle that circumscribed Kierkegaard's nature must then be obtained by psychological intuition, and its aspect might be in danger of being marked by its author's personal sympathies or antipathies. Of course it was not to be expected that a man of Brandes' temperament and views would be able to or would wish to escape this danger, and that he did not do so is now obvious to everybody. And as it might also be anticipated, it was the positive, religious side of Søren Kierkegaard's nature that Brandes failed to understand; he branded it with the word reverence, and he himself emphasised the worldly character of the nature of reverence: "Reverence is something quite different from piety, though these words are literally the same[1]; reverence eschews criticism, it purposely breaks its critical weapons" (p. 33). There can hardly be any doubt that Brandes resorted to a pious fraud for the benefit of the cause he served, when he reduced Kierkegaard's religious disposition to a mere tendency to subjection, faith in authority, etc.; as is well known, it has been proved that Brandes, better than most people, knew the religious power of Kierkegaard's writings (P. V. Rubow "Georg Brandes Briller" Chapter 4 § 1). The error therefore does not afford grounds for testing Georg Brandes' psychological faculties, but proves that we are justified in ranging his book on Søren Kierkegaard among the semi-agitatorial works. The strange, not uninteresting transition from the Christian faith to an aristocratic radicalism which Brandes asserted to be the line followed by Kierkegaard's spiritual development, can be traced back to his too external interpretation of Kierkegaard's relation to religion. It precluded the correct explanation, which essentially changes the direction of the movement, that gradually as the visible range of Søren Kierkegaard's reverence decreased, the intensity of his relation to God increased.

Through this mistake Brandes made Kierkegaard another than he was, and thereby, and by his method, the leading principle of which was simplification, made Kierkegaard's nature simpler, more platitudinous, less dialectically complicated than it was, and thus robbed the strong concrete realistic impressions of their true sounding-board, and ascribed to them an independent crucial significance for Søren Kierkegaard's development. That disproportion appears most clearly in his explanation of the history of the engagement. This was the fact that made Kierkegaard a poet, Brandes declares, and is so fortunate as to be able to refer to Kierkegaard's own statement in "The Point of View for my Work as an Author", but also finds himself in the situation of being compelled to skim over the remarks: "It was a dual fact.———I became a poet: but with

---

1. The Danish term for reverence is "pietet" and for piety "fromhed".

my leanings towards religion, nay with my decided religiousness, the same fact also became a religious awakening, so that in the most crucial sense I came to understand myself in religion, in that religiousness to which my attitude had been as towards a possibility. The fact made me a poet; had I not been the man I was, and the event, on the other hand, what it was, and had I not behaved as I did, nothing more would have come of it; I should have become a poet and then after many years have entered into a relation to religion. But precisely because I was so religiously developed as I was, the fact went much deeper and in a certain sense, in religious impatience, destroyed what I had become; being a poet destroyed it; or at any rate, all at once, I came to begin in two places at the very same time, though in such a way that being a poet was really something that did not concern me, was what I had become by means of something else—whereas the religious awakening was probably not what I had become by myself, but what I had become after my Ego, that is to say: in the fact that I was a poet I did not recognise myself in a deeper sense, but I did in the religious awakening." (13, 609-10).—By this addition his rupture with Regine assumes a double significance, partly as a cause, and partly as a mere Socratic occasion to restore the proper relation between the internal and the external factors. Brandes, however, persists in his view that the betrothal is the decisive event in Søren Kierkegaard's youth (102), it is the creative formula for the writings that follow, and likewise the first basic theme (101), a primary constitutive element in the whole of the pseudonymous production (101) from "Either-Or" to and including "Unscientific Postcript", and he undertakes to prove it by showing that the crisis of the betrothal was the constantly repeated theme in the first phase of Kierkegaard's authorship (p. 82). But even when this project is well executed it does not prove anything but that the story of the betrothal was, indeed, the preferred theme in the production, not that it was its creative formula.

From these erroneous premises Brandes consistently drew fallacious conclusions, which he then had to read into the actual works at hand. It appears with all plainness from the otherwise so flexible and famous explanation of "Fear and Trembling", which begins with the ingenious rediscovery of the story of the betrothal in spite of the disguise, but ends in the astonishing remark that the critical reader will perceive that Søren Kierkegaard, while singing the praises of Abraham, is in reality idealising his own conduct at a critical moment (p. 109-10)—an unexpected misconception because Brandes, in connection with his analysis, quotes the passage from the diary which, if it has once been set in its proper context, should show clearly that "Fear and Trembling" is a judgment passed on Kierkegaard's own actions. "Had I had faith, I should have stayed with Regine". Søren Kierkegaard, like Johannes de Silentio only mastered the movement of infinite resignation, while Abraham, the true champion of faith, was able to carry out the dual movement of infinity. On the other hand, the misconception is a natural consequence of the fact that the history of the betrothal is regarded as the primary constitutive element of the works; by this view Brandes prevented himself from discovering Søren Kierkegaard's dialectical attitude towards his own book and his humble admission of his own inferiority to the father of belief.

Rubow's elevation of the book about Søren Kierkegaard to "by far the cleverest and most objectively penetrating book written by Brandes", must be regarded as qualified praise; the scientific value of Brandes' contribution to Kierkegaard research is so far beyond doubt; but his objectivity only appears when it is viewed from a favourable angle. But what his book has lost in truth it has gained in beauty. It is a poetical interpretation of Søren Kierkegaard's life and works, and as such translucent and refulgent as crystal, a masterly and brilliant paraphrase of the history of a genius.

Fifteen years later, in 1892, Harald Høffding issued his short publication "Søren Kierkegaard som Filosof". (Søren Kierkegaard, the Philosopher). Harald Høffding (1843-1931) who from 1883 to 1915 was professor of philosophy in the University of Copenhagen, in several respects shared Brandes' opinions, on one point his fate, too. Like Brandes he passed through a prolonged religious crisis in his youth under the influence of Kierkegaard's writings. But in his temper and attitude towards life he was a contrast to Brandes, a moderate and lustreless thinker; his extensive and valued production is sustained by the endeavour to demonstrate continuity in thought and history, and his feeling towards life found final expression in "the great humour", that belief in the survival of value which reconciles us to vicissitudes and personal defeats.

Høffding's book about Kierkegaard forms a similar contrast to that of Brandes as Sainte-Beuve's literary method to that of Taine. In Brandes' book the individual history constitutes the straight line of evolution on to which the works can be projected, but Høffding's book is composed in the semblance of a target, where Kierkegaard's basic philosophical thoughts form the centre and each of the surrounding circles represents a group of conditional factors. Høffding, like Taine, is a determinist and follows him in grouping the determining circumstances under three heads: race, environment, and period of time. Against a continuation of Taine's theory, the doctrine of the dominant quality, he knew how to guard himself.

The situation in intellectual history at the time of Kierkegaard (the moment) derived its character from the romantic-speculative philosophy of religion, the greatest names of which were Schleiermacher and Hegel. Though disagreeing in many details, these thinkers had in common the conviction of harmony between faith and knowledge. What nourished the religious feeling, could, transformed into ideas, be made accessible to the intellect. In Denmark this optimistic philosophy found adherents in Heiberg and Martensen, though the latter showed a somewhat suspicious independence by combining speculation with theology, but it had opponents too, among them Sibbern and Poul Møller, who were not only contemporaries of Søren Kierkegaard but also personal acquaintances of his. They launched that reaction against Hegel to which Kierkegaard was later to give such pertinent expression.—In the chapter on Kierkegaard's personality his dependence on race and environment is shown. "We are beckoned beyond himself, back to his family and his race and to the traditions that formed the spiritual atmosphere of his childhood" (p. 28), says Høffding, and it appears from these words that the term „environment" is used in a narrower sense here than in Taine. In the melancholy which was inherent in his race (West Jutland) and his disposition, which was fostered by his upbringing, Høffding sees the crucial element of Søren Kierkegaard's personality. It is interpreted as the psychological cause of the two basic impulses, reverence and contempt, with which Brandes operated. His contempt is the reaction of the ever-anxious against the frivolous, his reverence and uncritical respect for the Christian religion expresses the melancholy yearning, melancholy to madness, for a firm hold in the confusion of existence. In addition to these passions Høffding finds other elements in Kierkegaard's nature which can be derived neither from his race nor his melancholy; these are a faculty for dialectical thought, imagination, and an energetic will to concentrate, to bend his qualities to work for a cause. This not very surprising picture of Søren Kierkegaard is stated to have been formed from the entries in diaries from Kierkegaard's youth; there can hardly be any doubt that actually it was formed from impressions of the whole of the man Søren Kierkegaard, and merely confirmed by the entries in the diaries. Hence it would seem less suitable to be used again to explain the production.

With these preliminaries Høffding pursues a double purpose. At the same time as he describes the inner and outer circumstances that had an essential share in Søren Kierkegaard's thought, he purports to give the conditions for isolating what is of lasting value. "I am convinced that just as the figures that leave an ideal impression on our minds, come into existence under definite psychological and historical circumstances, so also their ideal significance is not weakened—if it be really present—by their being viewed in their definite limitation and conditionateness. On the contrary, it is absolutely necessary to demonstrate the latter, if we are to be able to separate the lasting value from what may be due to fleeting and purely individual circumstances" (p. 2). This means then that when it has been pointed out in what respects Søren Kierkegaard's thoughts have been dependent on accidental historical and personal circumstances, the part of his activities which will survive and be effective after his death can be arrived at by simple subtraction.

In accordance with the statement in the introduction and the procedure in the first three chapters we then expect first an exposition of Kierkegaard's philosophy in which it is explained in its individual and historical limitation, bound in its implications (by reverence) to the Christian dogmatics and in its further elaboration dependent on the speculative fashion of the day, and then an evaluation of the bearing of this philosophy on positivist thinking. But here Høffding disappoints the just expectations of his readers. Already in his survey of Kierkegaard's thoughts he arranges them on positivist principles and merely mentions them in so far as they correspond to a problem in the unconditioned human philosophy. In doing so Høffding breaks the continuity in his own book. In the first part he employs a method which should make historical research as objectively reliable as a natural scientific investigation; its starting point is the universal laws, its primary aim, understanding; and its means a reconstruction of the causal chain in which the literary phenomenon was the last link. This praiseworthy impersonal attitude should of course also have marked the middle chapters of the book, the characterisation of Kierkegaard's philosophy, and Høffding's own opinions should only have been presented in the final evaluation of Kierkegaard's activity. But in the central part of the book the two thinkers' domains overlap; Kierkegaard's qualitative dialectic is subordinated to Høffding's quantitative dialectic. This mistake is expressed already in the inverse course of Høffding's exposition of Kierkegaard's ideas. He passes from Kierkegaard's criticism to its derived result: his relation to God; it is inferred from his scepticism, whereas the fact was that his scepticism was in great part rooted in his religious and moral conception of the world.

Søren Kierkegaard's theory of knowledge, Høffding explains, was directed against speculation, which imagined it could grasp absolute reality; thought, Kierkegaard asserted, cannot reach reality without converting it into imagined reality. Laws can be given for thinking, a logical system, but existence cannot be reduced to a system, partly because we and it are in being, partly because there is a chasm between thinking and being. The inmost nature of being is, then, incomprehensible to the human mind, it is paradoxical; and disquieted by objective uncertainty, the existing being postulates the existence of God in self-defence and passionately insists on the subjective truth of this idea. After arriving at this result, that truth is subjective, Søren Kierkegaard reverses the proposition: subjectivity is truth, i.e. only that is truth which is acquired with energy and passion.—As the starting point for his description of Søren Kierkegaard's ethics Høffding takes Kierkegaard's contention, dealt with especially in "The Concept of Dread", that man's spiritual development is not continuous as is the organic, but happens by leaps and bounds from quality to quality, a view which stirs up Høffding to lengthy protests. These leaps appear everywhere in Kierkegaard's ethics and are implied in his exposition of the stages of life. To a humanistic consideration the possible forms of existence succeed gradually to each other; Søren Kierkegaard, however, groups them in three classes, the æsthetic, the ethical, and the religious, which are sharply separated from each other by an inexplicable qualitative transition, a leap. Life in these three different stages is determined respectively by the relation to what is possible, the relation to reality, and the relation to God. The higher the dispensation under which man lives, the greater is the burden imposed on him, the greater are the contrasts which he is to unite in his existence. As a designation for those who are able to meet the claims of the higher stages Kierkegaard introduces the category of "the single individual", expressing the idea that the individual only knows himself, his own heart, which therefore harbours his tasks and ethical reality; the category corresponds to subjectivism in Kierkegaard's theory of knowledge. The scale of ethical values underlying the stages set up, is, asserts Høffding, purely formal, "it is the degree of tension which determines the height of the standard"; hence the paradoxical religiousness (i.e. the Christian religion which constitutes the last formation in the religious stage) is the last and highest level of existence; there the contrasts are the greatest, there comes the claim of a breach with things temporal; the demand of being dead to the world; a demand which can only be complied with by man during the most painful inner tension.

A characteristic example of how greatly Høffding transforms and reduces Kierkegaard's thoughts by his qualitative dialectic is found in his treatment of the leap. By introducing this category into philosophy Kierkegaard, according to Høffding, defined himself as an intellectual type. In the history of philosophy there occur two kinds of thinkers, the analytic and the synthetic, and Søren Kierkegaard belongs to the former, who dissolve coherences and break up the transitions which the synthetic nature has established. But, Høffding explains, the profound dissimilarity between these types is only apparent, in reality they are, respectively, the happy and the unhappy votaries of the same ideal. "He (S.K.) too felt a passionate need of understanding. And indeed his whole strong stressing of the paradox, of the irrational, of the sudden jerk that destroys the continuity would be incomprehensible if he did not himself feel a desire for retaining the continuity. His doctrine of truth as a paradox, expresses that this desire has been disappointed" (p. 73). Thus the philosophies of quality and quantity are mediated. But the mutually antagonistic theories of breach and continuity point back to a deeper antagonism than the relative one between the analytic and synthetic thinkers. In the relation between Kierkegaard and Høffding the disagreement can at any rate be traced to the fundamental disagreement in principle between the dualistic and the monistic view of the world. And the dualism manifested in Kierkegaard's sudden leap is grounded in the postulate which his religious conviction bid him accept, that man is by nature a synthesis of the finite and the infinite, of the temporal and the eternal, of necessity and freedom. The mission of man is to let the eternal pervade and dominate the temporal, thus freeing the individual entirely from the power of the latter. As the eternal part of man manifests itself the breach takes place. The faith in which this sudden leap ends thus includes a belief in human nature's original affinity with God (cf. T. Bohlin, Søren Kierkegaards etiska åskådning, p. 109). This conviction of Kierkegaard's as to the divine origin of the human soul is, however, not only lacking in Høffding's account of the concept of the sudden leap, but the leading ideas both in Søren Kierkegaard's theory of knowledge and in his stages: subjectivity and the single individual, cannot be rightly understood without it. What makes the movement of subjectivity, of intensity, true is not that it leads away from human fellowship to loneliness and pain, but that literally and actually it leads nearer to God. "God is subject and therefore only for subjectivity in intensity" (7,185).

With the large chapter on Kierkegaard's philosophy Høffding had actually completed the plan he had laid for his work. The framework of the plan had been filled out, though not in a quite satisfactory way. The fifth and last chapter, which neither with respect to viewpoint nor method forms a continuation of the rest of the book, must then be regarded as a second part, if not actually as an independent treatise. It covers the time from 1847 to 1885, and it aims at showing the connection between Kierkegaard's religious (in specie Christian) development in the years immediately following the termination of the religious production and the passionate attack he launched on the church and the clergy in the last ten months before his death. The same subject had been treated by the literary and religious historian HANS SOPHUS VODSKOV (1846-1910) in 1881 in an article in Illustreret Tidende (XXII, 1881): "En Krise i Søren Kierkegaards Liv" (A Crisis in Søren Kierkegaard's Life, reprinted in 1884 in Spredte Studier 1-30, to which the references that follow apply).

The reason why the old question as to the relation between Kierkegaard's religious writings and his drastic pamphlet polemics, which had been so animatedly debated in newspapers and periodicals after his death, was again taken up for discussion was that an answer had in the meantime become possible; the last volumes of Kierkegaard's posthumous papers, covering the period 1848-1855, appeared in 1880-81. This provided the material for filling the gap in the history of Kierkegaard's development. It was this material that Vodskov and Høffding worked with, each with his own result. A survey of their treatises will take the shape of a comparative study; this procedure will prove useful in judging the methods employed by them.

Vodskov's view of the case is as follows. In the year 1849 Søren Kierkegaard underwent a spiritual crisis, the germ of which was apparently only a small problem, whether he should publish the three papers he had completed in 48, "Preparation for a Christian Life", "The Sickness unto Death", and "The Point of View for my Work as an Author", and if so, whether it should be under his own name. But the question went deep, for if he did as he had intended in 48, if he published the papers without any pseudonym in spite of their hostile attitude to the existing conditions, then he would have broken with the prevalent form of Christianity and assumed the guise of a reformer and would then perhaps be exposed to the lot of a witness to the truth, martyrdom, while he had really hoped that God would take away his melancholy so that he could apply for a living and so amongst other things restore his tottering finances. His inmost doubt then was whether he was really called to be a witness to the truth or was merely a poet. "This is— — —the nerve of the whole movement, that he has reached his limit, that he has become doubtful as to his call, uncertain as to his duty, uncertain as to God's intention with him" (p. 13). The result was that Kierkegaard mediated, i.e. he rewrote "The Point of View" and published the other two books semi-pseudonymously. In the years that followed he trained himself in his strict view of Christianity without as usual reproducing his own development in his writings; he had understood that "Christianity is not to produce, but to exist". For four years he refused to yield to his inclination to produce; and this is the obvious reason for "The Moment". His natural outlet thus barred, his idea of reform grew powerful, and Martensen's proclaiming of Mynster as a witness to the truth was to Kierkegaard reason enough to throw down the pen for good and seize the judge's sword.—Vodskov's opinion of this development was that in 1849 Kierkegaard swerved from his main line, led astray by his striving for personal truth. Had he followed his calling, which was to be and to remain a poet, his production would have fallen into three groups, each with its own theme for poetic treatment: 1843-46, the movement of intensity towards Christianity, 1847-48, the persecution of the Christian in the world, and from 1849, the glorification of the religious life. But as he became engrossed in the austerity of original Christianity it dawned on him that Mynster's Christianity was untrue, and the perception of this suggested to him quite a different conception of his work, and in conflict with his original view and his whole nature he transformed himself into a passionate and monotonous agitator for the re-introduction of Christianity in the Christian world. Attempts to explain his activities as an author as the realisation of a single plan according to which the first act brings Christianity into view, the second act presents Christianity in its ideal austerity, while the third act then on this basis passes judgment on the existing, will go aground on the profound crisis in 49 and the hesitation and vacillation of the following six years.

Quite another picture of Kierkegaard's development in the years prior to the church storm will be found in Høffding's treatise. There the above-mentioned movement away from the church is not traced to a crisis but on the contrary to a religious experience, a Christian awakening. In the Easter of 1848 Kierkegaard writes in his diary: "Now I have reached faith in the deepest sense— — —. To God everything is possible; this thought is now in the deepest sense my watchword, has acquired a significance for me which I had never imagined." In his later entries in his diaries from 48 and 49 Kierkegaard often refers back to this time as a crucial turning point. This change of heart gave him a keener eye for the austerity of the Christian ideals and the weakness of the Christian church; at the same time his respect for his own time had been destroyed, in the first place during the persecution of the Corsair, when he was made a laughing stock to the man in the street and the mighty had left him to fight for the common welfare alone, but also during the political commotion in 48, when those in power, particularly Mynster, showed a grave want of authority. The internal and external conditions for hostile action were thus present, but for several reasons it was some years before it materialised. For the question of the publication of his religous writings from 48 involved him in lengthy deliberations on his own personal attitude to Christianity and they ended in the clear admission: "I confess that I am not in the strict sense a witness to the truth"; and Høffding adds to this: "It was in reality a fight concerning the witness to the truth which he was fighting with himself long before the great public controversy on the subject broke out— — —the external struggle is seen plainly here as a continuation of the internal one. This is always the case when a battle is fought with authority and earnestness" (p. 134). After this Høffding continues his exposition with an account of the historical events and the ideas in Kierkegaard's polemics. Høffding also was no absolute admirer of Kierkegaard's last works, but what Vodskov only mentions in passing, that Søren Kierkegaard was "hopelessly blind to the historical aspect of the case" (p. 28) Høffding takes as his main objection: that the Christianity of the New Testament does not exist, and did not exist in Søren Kierkegaard's time finds its good explanation in the fact that "the nearness of the kingdom is part of the original Christian teaching and underlies the evaluation of all the circumstances and tasks of life in the New Testament" (p. 154); after the futile waiting for 1900 years, this implication of the gospels had fallen away, and the doctrine cannot then be preached unaltered.

Vodskov and Høffding used the same method for their treatises, which is no wonder, as they drew on the same material, the diaries, with the same object, to find the psychological explanation of Kierkegaard's transformation from a poet philosopher to an agitator; it is all the more peculiar that their results differ widely; the reason for this must at the outset be supposed to be a flaw in the method. The latter is very simple, briefly it is this: with a knowledge of the historical truth to go back in time to rediscover it as a psychological possibility; in the present case this means that, while keeping in mind our knowledge of Søren Kierkegaard's factual external change at the turn of the year 1854-55, we must peruse the diaries of the preceding years and select from them and collocate the entries which testify to the corresponding change of heart. The method may be good enough in its way, especially when applied to Søren Kierkegaard who entered even the least stir of his soul; but it cannot be denied that it requires agreement in the evaluation of historical facts. And here is the salient point where Vodskov and Høffding part. Vodskov declares that he is no admirer of "The Moment": "It seems to me to be one of the poorest of his works in thought and rather more brutal than brilliant in its form, whereas I have in many ways drawn nourishment particularly from the first series of his writings until 48" (p. 20). Høffding on the other hand, though he complains a little of Kierkegaard's fierceness, still looks upon the whole controversy with the church with the greatest interest and awe at Kierkegaard's contribution. "The dispute which was here provoked and to which our literature knows no equal, if we consider the greatness of the theme and the passion with which it was carried on by those who had started it, I will not try to describe in detail— — —. It is a quarrel of the same kind as that between Plato and the Sophists, and between Pascal and the Jesuits.— — —It would be a great mistake if one read them (i.e. Søren Kierkegaard's contributions) merely with an æsthetic interest in the violent polemics; mighty words are spoken of the relation between ideal and self-deception which have a message to every one, whatever his stand" (p. 114).—Above we remarked that the method here employed was especially applicable to Søren Kierkegaard on account of the fullness of the notes in his diaries; but on the other hand it is a danger the moment it can depend on a subjective judgment what one may expect to find in them; in the rich material we find what we are searching for; even if our search is unjustified; but then the find will often merely reflect our own unjustified expectation. In "The Moment" Vodskov saw decay and showed that its origin was a long and exhausting crisis with a sad issue; to Høffding the writings seemed to bear the impress of grandeur and might, when he read them he heard the trump of history and he found their source in the awakening to Christianity in which Søren Kierkegaard's development culminated.

P. A. Heiberg's searching inquiry into the same period of Kierkegaard's history has in all essentials confirmed Høffding's right to regard the crisis as a mere pause, and the awakening to Christianity as the decisive event in the last part of Søren Kierkegaard's life. Thus the honour of having called attention to the great change in the Easter of 48 and having attached so much importance to it is indisputably Høffding's; he could do so because he himself was a man with a theological past who had had his trials and therefore could distinguish pathos from euphony; but in method his work is on a line with Vodskov's which led to a fallacious result; thus Høffding's treatise does not possess an independent objective reliability but derives an essential part of its value from later research.

3. Waldemar Rudin, P. A. Heiberg

As is well known, Brandes' book on Kierkegaard was an adaptation of a series of lectures he had given in the autumn of 1876 in Denmark, Norway, and Sweden; on his route through Scandinavia he was followed at the time by clergymen and professors of divinity, weeding out the tares he had sown. Among these was the Swedish theologian Waldemar Rudin (1833-1921, professor in the University of Uppsala 1877-1900), who in the spring of 1877 delivered some "counter"-lectures in Uppsala; he recast them into the book "Søren Kierkegaard's Person and Production", which appeared in 1880.

Among ecclesiastical Kierkegaard researchers there was long a tradition of praising Rudin whenever occasion offered; to him was allotted so much more recognition than he deserved as had been unjustly withheld from Brandes. Amongst other things it was said that between the nature of Rudin himself and Kierkegaard there was a profound affinity which made him specially qualified to penetrate into the maze of Kierkegaard's production, while as late as after the turn of the century his book was regarded as incomparably the best about Søren Kierkegaard as a Christian writer. The motives for this judgment are not quite clear, but in addition to deliberate culture-political intentions it is no doubt marked by that confusion with respect to the viewpoint for Kierkegaard research which has so long prevailed. Rudin was the first Scandinavian enquirer who tried to take Kierkegaard's self-analyses seriously; this placed him in such a relation to the production that the edifying aspect and that only, came into view. This choice emanating from an ingenuous conviction that Søren Kierkegaard himself was bound to know best how his production was to be understood, was confounded with congeniality, and it was further inferred that Rudin's picture of Søren Kierkegaard was the right one, though somewhat too appreciative, while that of Brandes was wrong even though it was very brilliant. A direct comparison between the two books would not, however, be just, the different points of view from which they were written must be taken into account, as well as the fact that Søren Kierkegaard himself had classed his exposition under one of them.

As far as Rudin is concerned, the idea of basing the description of Kierkegaard's works on his autobiographical records was not even his own; he had taken it from Pastor Bärthold of Halberstadt, who already as early as 1873 published "Søren Kierkegaard, eine Verfasserexistens eigner Art, aus seinen Mitteilungen zusammengestellt", a small book the main contents of which are extracts from "The Point of View for my Work as an Author". Hence Rudin's book is in no respect original in its plan; nevertheless we cannot deny that it has value, and we must concede to its author, in addition to enthusiasm, a talent for reading and reporting. The fact that his work on Kierkegaard, which had been planned to fill two volumes, never got beyond the first and easiest, would seem to indicate that he himself did not feel capable of doing more. The first volume available contains "a condensed historical survey of Kierkegaard's life and activity as an author"; its main sources are the chapter "Reference to a simultaneous trend in Danish literature" in "Unscientific Postcript"; the passages in the posthumous papers where Kierkegaard mentions his own productions; but chiefly "The Point of View". The promised second volume was to "endeavour to answer certain main questions with a view to judging him rightly, namely these: "What he actually was as an author and a person", further "What had made him what he was": and finally "What is required in order to understand and judge him" (p. 13).

Rudin's talent for reporting does not indeed reveal itself either in the first or the last chapter of his book which deal, respectively, with the beginning and the end of Kierkegaard's activities as a religious author. Rudin had to prepare them without any prompting from the master, so they lack inner cohesion and concentration on the essential point. This applies especially to Chapter 1, in which, as far as possible, all the more significant impressions from that part of Kierkegaard's life which precedes "Either-Or" are recorded on 14 pages. This part is based on Brandes' description of the same period of Kierkegaard's life, but that clear and sharp picture has been touched up from a Christian point of view and encumbered with dates and details. The seventh and last chapter chiefly contains reprints of the bitter articles which Kierkegaard and his antagonists exchanged in the heat of the Church contest. Rasmus Nielsen's edition of the newspaper articles gave him the contents; Rudin's own contribution is confined to short instructive remarks inserted between the lengthy quotations; he has made no attempt to give a synthetic representation of the historical events.

In the five remaining chapters his powers are displayed to advantage. Here he has really succeeded in outlining the structure of the Gothic building which Kierkegaard asserted that he had erected. The soaring style and the multitude of details have been preserved in spite of the simplification. Chapter 2 deals with "Either-Or", the transition from the æsthetic to the ethical stage; Chapter 3 with the continued ascent towards paradoxical religiousness. These two chapters together form a parallel to the fourth on the "Unscientific Postcript" where the way from speculation to the Christian outlook is described; the common aim of the two lines of development is to point forward towards the goal of personally becoming a Christian, the form they have in common is the indirect communication. In Chapters 5 and 6 Rudin gives an account of the two periods of purely religious production separated by the year 48, when Søren Kierkegaard's thoughts came to a head in his polemical writings. These chapters contain records of the works in which direct communication is employed and together with the three previous ones comprise the whole enormous religious production which arose from the æsthetic "Either-Or" and finally with "Discourses at the Communion on Fridays" came to rest at the foot of the altar.

A more detailed review of Rudin's book will be superfluous; what applies to the book as a whole also applies to its separate parts and parts of parts. The exposition is most solicitously kept in harmony with Kierkegaard's own commentaries on his work, and it has not been noticed that these commentaries do not agree with each other; the account of the individual books is "exact and on the whole dialectically reliable"; at most then Rudin's book—including the introductory and the final chapter—contains what Søren Kierkegaard himself held that he had expressed in his works. Søren Kierkegaard's own interpretation is then not only the subject of Rudin's work but also its limit. Beyond this he does not go, nor does he make any attempt to do so, and Rudin's treatise can hardly be regarded as anything but a compendium of Søren Kierkegaard's discursive activities. As such it has indeed considerable value; and viewed against the background of the other Kierkegaard research of the time it constitutes an important corrective. Søren Kierkegaard's contention that he had employed a form of intellectual communication derived particularly from Socrates was dismissed as a later, or at any rate a late, invention, and his consequent demand not to be made responsible for the statements of the pseudonyms was therefore disregarded and the arrangement with the invented names was designated as a literary mannerism. Rudin deserves credit for proving that the knowledge of the existing thinker's special form of communication can be used as a starting point for an account of his activities which with respect to clarity and inner coherence does not fall far short of the viewpoint which explains Søren Kierkegaard's writings from his life.

Akin to Rudin by his love of Søren Kierkegaard and by his trust in the truth of the author's pronouncements, but at the same time quite different from him by his independence and originality was P. A. HEIBERG. His epoch-making work as editor of Kierkegaard's papers and interpreter of the history of his development will presently be dealt with more fully. Prior to the large connected work which was begun around 1907 came the publication of a small book, "Bidrag til et psykologisk Billede af Søren Kierkegaard i Barndom og Ungdom" (Contributions towards a Psychological Portrait of Søren Kierkegaard in Childhood and Youth, 1895) which differs decidedly from his later books by its method and free-and-easy, almost undergraduate-like tone. Although this first book, by its subject, too, seemed to lay a foundation, it was not on this that he continued to build. So as to procure a basis for his understanding of the development of Søren Kierkegaard's character in his maturer years, Heiberg tried to form a picture of Kierkegaard as a young man, and in order that this portrait should not show traces of a later knowledge of Søren Kierkegaard and his public activities, he took as his starting point the documents written by the headmaster Michael Nielsen about the schoolboy Søren Kierkegaard, one testimonial written in Danish which deals with Kierkegaard but seems rather to refer to the "curly-headed Fritz", and another testimonial in Latin, in which his home and especially his father are made the subject of eulogy. As far as is possible Michael Nielsen's words are then accepted as true, but the assertion that as a boy Søren Kierkegaard was openhearted and reckless is so much at variance with the traditional conception and with Kierkegaard's own interpretation of his childhood that a supplement is necessary. Heiberg finds this in "The Point of View", that "Report to History" the objectiveness of which he regarded as "grand" in 1895. The thing now to be done was to make the gloomy conception of Kierkegaard's boyhood and youth from the "The Point og View" harmonise with the bright view of the testimonial; this could not be done without quibbling. For the Søren Kierkegaard whom Michael Nielsen knew was open to everything that invited special interest, cheerful, goodnatured, unspoilt, an openhearted but possibly a slightly reckless character; while Søren Kierkegaard remembers about himself that already as a boy he had fallen a prey to a heavy melancholy. It was due to his early developed tendency to reflection which burned out his spontaneity; it drew its strength from his imagination which made this spontaneity ideally present to him though he had in reality lost it by his reflection, and finally it became so persistent because he possessed a demoniac power of hiding it behind an apparent happiness and gaiety. In the picture that Heiberg can draw of Søren Kierkegaard's mind Michael Nielsen's description is then reduced, for the time being, to apply to that aspect only of Søren Kierkegaard's nature which was turned towards the outer world. It is a deceptive outer shell which has been consciously put on in order to conceal a terrible melancholy. But his melancholy is a sympathetic melancholy, that is to say, a melancholy which has not engendered a hatred of God and man, but the intensity of which is due precisely to a profound love of life. And this love, which lies still deeper than the melancholy, can without constraint be brought to agree with Nielsen's contention that Søren was goodnatured and unspoilt.—Thus then Heiberg found three strata in what he called the young Kierkegaard's psychic machinery: outermost the frank young fellow whom his headmaster Nielsen saw and described, then the melancholy demon of reticence, which probably very few contemporaries divined behind the apparent lightheartedness, and in his inmost heart the idols: good-nature and innocence. In order to obtain a more complete impression of the young Kierkegaard Heiberg now wanted to fill in the outline he had drawn with individual vivifying features and for that purpose he tried to find "more concrete determinations of the separate links in the psychic machinery of whose structure", he thought, "he had gained a psychological understanding in the abstract by means of the information from "The Point of View" (p. 29). As an objective scientific enquirer he must then first on the basis of the results already obtained put precise questions. These we shall here quote, adding a condensed account of the answers, for which Heiberg collected material from Søren Kierkegaard's works, from his diaries, and from the available statements of his contemporaries.

(1) The question as to the relation of his melancholy to physical

causes. For the solution of this problem, which Heiberg never succeeded in clearing up, he could only in 1895 refer to that disproportion of soul and body which Kierkegaard sometimes mentioned in his diary, and which Heiberg explains as a disproportion between Søren Kierkegaard's large strong head and his small slight body.

(2) The question as to the relation of his reticence to his good-nature and innocence. Kierkegaard's reticence must in great part have consisted in veneration for his father who had transferred his melancholy to his son not only through his blood but also by tradition; that this veneration was so great as to conquer his sympathy with men was due to the fact that Søren Kierkegaard thought he owed his faith in God to his father.

(3) The question as to what concrete impressions, altogether, Søren Kierkegaard received as a child and youth.—The reply to this question Heiberg divided into three parts, each of them corresponding to one of Kierkegaard's three stages of life; in all cases, however, it was from his father that Søren received the deepest and most enduring impressions. He influenced him æsthetically by displaying in his presence imagination and reflection intertwined, he exerted a tremendous ethical influence on him and his brothers and sisters by exacting responsibility and absolute obedience. Under these circumstances his upbringing only furthered Søren's spiritual development; with respect to religion his influence was of enormous strength, but not all to the good. He purposely taught his son that the love of Christ was despised and jeered at in the world, and so laid the foundation for the polemical element in Søren Kierkegaard's nature, which finally found expression in the category "the single individual"; but he also filled the boy's mind with a fear of Christianity by showing himself powerless—on one occasion—to live up to its demands, and uttering doubts as to his own salvation .

The curious method Heiberg employed in his first publication was no doubt developed under the negative influence of previous Kierkegaard research, more especially Brandes' treatise. He concludes his book with the declaration that its value should consist in giving psychological clues for the use and appraisal of the material for a biographical exposition of Kierkegaard's life,—and a concrete starting-point for a psychological description of Søren Kierkegaard's inner development; it will hardly be wrong to see in these pronouncements a polemical shaft aimed at his predecessors, who had used the published diaries in a rather arbitrary way and formed an impression of Søren Kierkegaard's inner life under the influence of their own sympathy for or antipathy to him. If we recall the point from which Brandes started in his description of Kierkegaard's development it will be clear that Heiberg's account of Kierkegaard's mental structure must be regarded as an attempt to arrive at a truer, a more objective image of the inner life of the great thinker than was given by Brandes, when he set up reverence and scorn as his ruling passions. The two enquirers set themselves the same task but employed different methods. Brandes tried, by psychological intuition, to form an idea of Kierkegaard's nature on the basis of the different, partly contradictory particulars that have come down to us, while Heiberg, in order to secure the objectivity of his exposition, first sought absolutely reliable documents from which he could extract by analysis the abstract outline of Søren Kierkegaard's mind, and filled out this diagram with concrete facts drawn in the main from Barfod's collection of materials, the individual notes and entries of which he now had the means of checking.

The scientific value of Heiberg's paper then in the first place depends on whether he has succeeded in procuring psychological material, the objective reliability of which may be regarded as beyond doubt. Heiberg, perhaps rightly, thought that Michael Nielsen's writings gave a trustworthy picture of the schoolboy Kierkegaard, whereas his assertion that the other and more important contribution to Kierkegaard's psychology, the autobiographical section of "The Point of View" was marked by a "grand, purely scientific objectivity" (p. 16) is as daring as it is ill-founded. Heiberg gives as the reason for his confidence in it that Kierkegaard in this book applies the standard of natural necessity to himself, which is at variance with his usual practice, and for that very reason testifies to a personal freedom of spirit guaranteeing the detachment of the exposition. This somewhat factitious argument had not, however, sufficient force to convince the reader in the long run of the reliability of "The Point of View", not even Heiberg himself. For Søren Kierkegaard's allegation that he had always been melancholy, that he had always realised that his melancholy was incurable, is most definitely contradicted by the papers from his youth .It was A. B. Drachmann who first pointed out this fact; and he drew the following conclusion from it: "It is in reality inconceivable that there should not in these records be found any trace of such a state of mind if it had been present; doubly inconceivable because there are so many expressions of quite another state of mind. To be sure Kierkegaard boasts that he knew how to conceal his melancholy from all others, but he had no reason to exclude it from his personal records, nor did he do so later on—quite the contrary. I cannot see better than that the deep shadows later cast over his life in his imagination also darkened the short time that was still free from them". (Udvalgte Afhandlinger pp. 197-98). To the unimpeachable logic of these lines Heiberg surrendered later on, but his psychological explanation of why "The Point of View's" conception of Kierkegaard's childhood and youth was partly misleading was again somewhat factitious: "The tendency of Kierkegaard to make the shadow of his melancholy blacker and blacker in the later years of his life and to let this shadow almost totally shroud not only his youth but also his childhood in a blackness of despair—this tendency, in my opinion, has its natural psychological explanation in the constantly increasing spiritual liberation from the power of melancholy which especially gathers impetus at and after the crisis intensifying his faith, which he underwent, plainly enough in the closest association with his writing of the decisive work "The Sickness unto Death", in the Easter week of 1848. It is the intensification of faith inaugurated with this crisis, and the consequent incipient recovery from melancholy that with a constantly stronger and surer feeling of liberation gives him power to draw the spectre of melancholy into the daylight, that monster which had hitherto weighed on him like a nightmare of darkness. It is the strong light from the relief afforded by the intensification of his faith in God, the strong light which in the entry of April 1848 so entirely overwhelms him, it is this that makes the shadow so black which he now lets his melancholy cast on his boyhood and youth." (A Segment pp. 55-56, cf. Helweg's "Søren Kierkegaard, A Psychologico-psychiatrical Study", pp. 32-33, agreeing with Drachmann and polemising against Heiberg).

That conviction of the truth of Kierkegaard's autobiography which Heiberg had in 1895 must then be regarded as a fruit of his deep and openly avowed admiration and affection for Kierkegaard and not as the result of a critical unfeeling research. Like Rudin, he was ardent, which does not make his book dull but subjective in its basis—in spite of all his striving after methodical objectivity.—A more detailed criticism of Heiberg's book is in so far unnecessary as it has been deprived of the foundation which is a necessary condition for the use of its special method; as a constructive whole the treatise will not survive, but regarded as a diplomatarium it still retains its value for any student of the young Kierkegaard.

4. Fredrik Petersen, Niels Téisen etc.

In a more remote relation to Søren Kierkegaard than the above-mentioned enquirers, all of whom have been personally worried by him and have been obliged to settle their personal account with him, we have a number of authors who seem to have expressed their opinions on Kierkegaard on behalf of institutions or parties rather than on their own behalf. Their understanding of him is often rather superficial, and in the majority of cases second-hand. It is a somewhat heterogeneous collection of persons with a theological training, whose activities as interpreters of Søren Kierkegaard should perhaps rather be ranged under a description of Kierkegaard's influence through the ages than under the history of Kierkegaard research. They approached Kierkegaard, each from his own ecclesiastical domain, without obtaining and without really seeking contact with him.

The earliest astir was Fredrik Petersen (1839-1903, Professor of systematic theology in the University of Oslo) whom Brandes' performance at Oslo in 1876 at once induced to deliver a series of lectures on Kierkegaard as a corrective. A year later he published a treatise on "Søren Kierkegaards Kristendomsforkyndelse" (Søren Kierkegaard's Teaching of Christianity), the greater part of which had previously been available to a smaller reading public in "Teologisk Tidsskrift for den evangelisk-lutherske Kirke i Norge" (1869 ff.). This mammoth work of 897 pages falls into three parts; the first part deals with Søren Kierkegaard's relation to the cultural and political tendencies that marked his time and thus gives the historical antecedents of his production, the individual works of which are quoted in the second part, and the ideas of which are given in a concentrated form and appraised in the last part. The main thesis of his work is that Søren Kierkegaard's production is a consistent reaction against Hegel. Hegel represented objectivity, Kierkegaard subjectivity, while Petersen represented virtue in the middle. Hegel started from a confidence in the natural faculty of cognition, Kierkegaard from "the clouded intellect", but Petersen himself argues from the reborn intellect. "It is true that the fall extinguished the light, but the revelation lit it again. In the revelation the standpoint is given from which insight into nature as well as into history can again be gathered to a whole, to the system of existence, which is fragmentary without it — —" (p. 482). What Petersen means by Kierkegaard's subjectivity appears from a 9-page compendium (527-36) of Kierkegaard's basic thoughts, given in the third part of the book. It is a mosaic of sentences from "Unscientific

Postcript", "Philosophical Fragments", "The Sickness unto Death" and others, halves and three-quarters of clauses, linked together by Petersen in periods. Here misapprehension and distortion come so thick upon each other that a consistent criticism would require an unreasonable amount of parallel quotations. But in brief it may, I think, be said that Søren Kierkegaard's religious ideal, the existing thinker, who feels spiritually bound to a transcendental reality and pledged to express his eternal experience in actual reality as existence, in Petersen's version has been deprived of contact with heaven as well as with earth. Both Kierkegaard's description of the ego (which in the state when it is without despair, is grounded transparently in the Power that constituted it (11, 145), and of the idealising passion (which anticipates the eternal in existence (7,300)), the two points of contact in Søren Kierkegaard's religious thought, are signally misunderstood, and his process of reflection is forced back upon itself so that it begins and ends in consciousness. His subjectivity therefore comes to mean isolation from God and man.

There is something almost contrary to nature about Petersen's book; it is a monster in volume and errors. No one before and no one after Petersen has documented his failure to understand Søren Kierkegaard at such length, nor with so much spirit confuted an imaginary Søren Kierkegaard on all fronts. And yet the book ends with a number of concessions to Søren Kierkegaard. The disproportion of the whole of this shadow fight taking place before our eyes is so formidable that we are compelled to believe that Petersen, in his secret heart, guessed at Søren Kierkegaard's real greatness.

Petersen's book dates from the beginning of the period; its first parts appeared at the same time as the first volumes of Søren Kierkegaard's posthumous papers, which in fact are not among its sources. The rest of the ecclesiastical literature about Kierkegaard came around the turn of the century, i.e. after the main works of the period had appeared. It gives nothing new but a number of variations on the themes already dealt with. Thus the year 1898 brought only 4 small books of markedly secondary character.—Showing most dependence on his predecessors, we have the Swede OSWALD KUYLENSTIERNA (1865-1932) whose book Søren Kierkegaard. Tänkaren och sanningssökaren. (The Thinker and Seeker after Truth), mostly a kind of anthology of selections from Brandes, Høffding, Rudin, and Heiberg with fragments of Kierkegaard's own works, is only of symptomatic interest.—A more independent attitude towards the contemporary Kierkegaard research is shown by the Danish clergyman CHRISTIAN JENSEN (1873-1949), who in his book on Søren Kierkegaards religiøse Udvikling (S. K.'s Religious Development) attempts, what is impossible in principle, to adopt Brandes' and Rudin's views at the same time.

In his main disposition Jensen follows Brandes and declares himself at one with his theory in the following words: His (Søren Kierkegaard's) development therefore does not take place through reflection but through experience. Not that his thoughts are inactive during his development, few have probably thought more or more acutely than Søren Kierkegaard, but each time he passes from one standpoint to another—not abandoning the previous one but passing into a higher stage where the old standpoint is included as a part only, i.e. gaining new ground for his Christian view of life—it is caused by an external event (p. 283).—The history of Søren Kierkegaard's religious development therefore can be divided into four chapters. Thus the first part of his activity as an author was due to "his father's last illness and death and his own engagement" (Chapters 2-9). In 1846 he took a higher line. The reason was the attack of the Corsair (10-12). The third stage was from 1848 and was due to the political events in that year (13-14), and finally the fourth and last was caused by Mynster's death and Bishop Martensen's funeral sermon (15-16).—In spite of his both practical and theoretical agreement with Brandes' genetic method Jensen tried to make the central part of his book (Chapters 3-14) a parallel to the section in Rudin (Chapters 2-6) in which the individual writings of Kierkegaard's production are analysed and inserted as links in the great chain, the first and last works of which were "Either-Or" and "Discourses at the Communion on Fridays". These two works are stated to be the poles in the movement which leads back from reflection to simplicity, from the indirect communication of the pseudonymous writings to the straightforward mode of expression in the religious writings. From a remark following immediately upon the above -quoted asseveration that Kierkegaard's spiritual development must be interpreted by his experience, it appears how Jensen thought he could combine the two antagonistic principles. "First he has his experience, then reflection sets in, and afterwards he discovers that he has experienced a fresh piece of Christian truth, which previously he indeed knew something about through his intellect, but which he has only now made his personal possession" (p. 283). This is the salient point, the question as to the relation of the external events to Kierkegaard's spiritual development. If the external experiences were accidental it is improbable that they should, by virtue of their own contents, force Søren Kierkegaard's thoughts to penetrate ever deeper into the Christian truth; that they did not do so was Brandes' view. If they did, we cannot regard them as accidental but the series of events must be supposed to bear some relation to Kierkegaard's mind as—consciously or unconsciously—selected from a multiplicity of impressions or, as Kierkegaard himself maintained and Rudin felt compelled to accept, as incidents which were deliberately provoked by Kierkegaard and the whole course of which was foreseen. Here of course he is thinking in the first place of the persecution by the Corsair coming in the middle of the authorship and dividing it into two. Søren Kierkegaard emphatically maintained his proprietary right to it; it was part of the plan, it was provoked when he changed his tactics. If this cannot be accepted we must also doubt the truth of his assertion of the one plan of the production and with that also the right to present the movement from "Either-Or" to the "Communion Discourses" as traversed or described uno tenore.—Christian Jensen emphatically asserts that the persecution by the Corsair came as a terrible and unexpected blow to Kierkegaard and gave him a new point of departure for his activity; nevertheless he shaped his exposition as a parallel to that of Rudin and in conclusion (pp. 245-46) quoted a lengthy passage from "On my Activity as an Author" where the unity of the movement is guaranteed. This position is untenable; he has retained Brandes' premisses but rejected the consequences and introduced Rudin's more Christian view instead.

Some months before the appearance of Jensen's book the Grundtvigian congregational minister Carl Koch (1860-1925) had published a diminutive paper on Søren Kierkegaard. It contained in a slightly enlarged form three lectures given the year before in meeting houses throughout the country, and now, at the easily understandable request of several of the audience, sent to press. This is popular reading in the best sense of the term, easy to follow, but probably difficult to write. In his view of Søren Kierkegaard Koch principally adhered to the opinions expressed by the humanists in the earliest phase of Kierkegaard research. The account in the first lecture of the connection between Kierkegaard's experience in his boyhood and youth (his father and his engagement) and the leading thoughts in the pseudonymous production (the intensity, the paradox, and the single individual) is directly traceable to Brandes; the explicit account in the second lecture of Søren Kierkegaard's development and production from the Corsair feud to his death exhibits a distinct dependence on Høffding's treatment of the same subject, and finally, for the last lecture, dealing with what he had most at heart, he drew on Vodskov's "A Crisis in Søren Kiergaard's Life". But though this treatise is the only one mentioned as a source, it is at the same time that of which Koch is most independent; he merely avails himself of its presentation of the problem in its main features. For in his last lecture he has an appraisal of Kierkegaard's fight against the Church, his work as a reformer, and as to this question Koch—like all other contemporary Kierkegaard enquirers—reserves his personal opinion.—In the year 1849 Søren Kierkegaard was in two minds about the question whether it was God's or man's fault that the Christianity of the New Testament did not exist, whether the ideal was too exalted or man too wicked. The problem had obtruded itself when he was thinking of publishing his polemical writings against the Church, and the solution he found, that of letting the books appear pseudonymously, not designating himself as a Christian but as a poet, showed that he had fallen into perplexity and self-contradiction. It meant that he merely wanted the ideal to be recognised, which is precarious for the advocate of existence. And the same perplexity, Koch thinks, asserted itself in Kierkegaard's last fight; he merely demanded the admission from the Church that it did not preach the ideal, not that its ministers were to be witnesses to the truth. And the reason for this uncertainty of Kierkegaard's, the reason why he quailed before the imitation of Christ, was that his peculiar and sad story had forced him into a false, non-evangelical, view of Christianity, hostile to life, had tied him to an ideal from which the best in his nature shrank. And because Christianity, as he preached it, was associated with an un-Christian asceticism, aloof from life, the Church could with reason brush aside his attack however much it might otherwise be in need of an awakener. "Kierkegaard had something of which the Church stood in need, but it could not receive it from his hand because it was mixed there with something it must rightly reject." (p. 131).

It appears with all clarity from the above quotation how largely Koch's positive Christian view of life influenced his understanding and judgment of Søren Kierkegaard's last fight. Høffding and Vodskov took objection to "The Moment" for historical and æsthetic reasons respectively, but Carl Koch, the preacher, could not shake off the inhuman demands of the pamphlets by a reference to the fact that Kierkegaard had betrayed his vocation as a poet or taught a doctrine which was merely suitable in a certain historical situation, but only by maintaining that Kierkegaard's Christianity was not that of the Gospels. This, then, he did; whether it is theologically justifiable shall not be discussed here, and probably no agreement will ever be reached on this point; but his indirect proof, that Kierkegaard's position in "The Moment" is obscure because he does not reply to the question whether the Christian ideal should be imitated, is no proof. The question is inspired by the Church; it cannot be answered in general, but only by the single individual. Søren Kierkegaard described the ideal, but without authority. From Christ, not from himself, the claim and the grace were to come.

The third and last of the Christian authors professing Christianity who in the year 1898 issued writings about Søren Kierkegaard was the Grundtvigian critic P. A. ROSENBERG (1858-1935). In his book "Søren Kierkegaard. Hans Liv, hans Personlighed og hans Forfatterskab. En Vejledning til Studiet af hans Værker". (His Life, his Personality, and his Production. A Guide to the Study of his Works) he again, as will appear from the title, examines Kierkegaard's history and production from the beginning to the bitter end. In his exposition of the various episodes of his life and in his account of his works Rosenberg drew very largely upon the books published in the period 1877-95; but his book differs from those of his predecessors by including the psychological explanation of all the conflicts and crises in Kierkegaard's life; in all its simplicity it is as follows: Søren Kierkegaard was an individualist; this is the secret of his personality which explains his life and his production.—By collating various statements from the first three chapters one can form an idea of how Rosenberg thought it had come to pass that Kierkegaard developed into an individualist and resolutely tried to maintain this doubtful position throughout his life. Søren Kierkegaard suffered from a melancholy that made him feel different from other people, isolated, solitary; and he could not by reflection arrive at a realisation of his relation to the community because his reflection was subordinate to his passion which again was inextricably bound up with his melancholy. Hence he became the single individual, and therefore he had to break off his engagement: "Kierkegaard was too much of an individualist for the relation to another person to become a vitally important relationship to him" (p. 32), hence the fundamental idea in his whole production became individualism (p. 39).—By his nature and by his type of mind Søren Kierkegaard was a pronounced idealist, but in his view of life he was a Christian; "both his bringing up, his father's influence, the unforgettable impression of the tragedy and sublime authority of Christianity and Kierkegaard's natural respect for authority all made him adhere firmly to the conviction of the divine origin of Christianity" (p. 69). That it to say, he had not chosen Christianity and individualism as the fundamental pillars of his view of life, they had been thrust upon him by inheritance and upbringing; therefore, and because he was not in the first place compounded of reflection but of passion he did not ask whether the two forms of life could be combined, but how they could be combined. Rosenberg thinks that he can trace back to this point the majority of misunderstandings and erroneous conclusions in Søren Kierkegaard's writings, and the self-contradictions in his final activity as a Christian revivalist, for in his opinion the task Kierkegaard had set himself was doomed to failure at the outset, "for in its essence Christianity is the religion of socialism; to regard it as individualistic is to distort all its values" (p. 69). The conclusion Rosenberg draws in his treatise will then be that Kierkegaard's mission was a failure in all essentials, and that his historical importance, if he has any such, will be that by his life he has proved once for all the impossibility of combining Christianity and individualism (p. 69. 209).

An author standing somewhat apart both by this general views and by his very limited sphere of interest is NIELS TEISEN, (1851-1916), a Danish headmaster and religious thinker. When we discussed Høffding's treatment of Kierkegaard's thought it was pointed out as a flaw in his exposition that it did not start from Kierkegaard's dogmatic views, and it was noted that Høffding's estimate of Søren Kierkegaard as a philosopher therefore lost its scientific validity. In order to remedy this defect Teisen, who in 1893 had written a small critical pamphlet against Høffding's book and amongst other things had given expression to a criticism of the same kind as the above-mentioned, published an explanation of Kierkegaard's Christian thought aiming to show his fundamental dependence on ecclesiastical dogmas. It appeared in 1903 and bore the title "On Søren Kierkegaard's Importance as a Christian Thinker", from which it will at once be seen that Teisen meant to use his insight into Kierkegaard's thought for a final and just judgment of his whole activity. This tendency to estimate and teach, which Teisen shares with the majority of his predecessors, but which was especially well-developed in him, spreads itself throughout the book at the expense of Kierkegaard. In the following record of Teisen's treatise his general reasoning will be disregarded in favour of the smaller part of the book dealing with the interpretation of Kierkegaard's thoughts and the account of their origin.

What characterised Søren Kierkegaard's relation to Christianity was his resolute accentuation of the ethical-practical aspect of the faith. To be a Christian was to him so connected with difficulties and anxieties with respect to the practical conduct of life that he could only to a slight extent occupy himself with the content of the faith. Hence his dogmatic reflections gathered round the few central, so-called soteriological, problems, the questions concerning human nature and the Saviour. Kierkegaard's conception of these very dissimilar creatures is to be found in "Philosophical Fragments" which to Teisen is the main source of knowledge about Kierkegaard's—not Johannes Climacus'—dogmatic views. The figure of Christ, Kierkegaard maintains, is a paradox; opposed definitions enter into it, open contradictions, the God and man, the eternal and the temporal; any one who wants to believe in Christ must therefore do so despite his understanding, by virtue of the absurd. And of man it is declared in the same place that he is "untruth"; natural man is absolutely different from God, without any power to realise or merely to seek the truth, utterly sunk in darkness, in total sin. The direct consequence of these views was the most rigid claims to man; it was man's Christian duty to renounce the use of his understanding, to destroy his joy in life which was evil at its root, to live as if dead. This conclusion is correct, Teisen maintains, and the premises accord with the orthodox theology. The doctrine of the paradox leads directly back in an unbroken line to the Athanasian symbol containing the assertion that Christ in himself combines two natures, a divine and a human nature. And the dogma of the absolute sinfulness of man Kierkegaard has adopted from Augustine; the doctrine of the latter, however, does not in principle belong to the teaching of the Protestant Church, though adhered to in reality, as will appear from the fact that the Church attributes to the new-born child original sin, which qualifies it for perdition.

Søren Kierkegaard's demand that the Christian should die to the world entirely agrees with orthodox theology, but, Teisen insists on his own account, orthodox theology does not agree with Christianity, and Søren Kierkegaard deserves credit for proving this. He did not do so by criticising or entering into controversies, but by applying the dogmas to life with strict consistency. He did not do it by attacking the orthodox faith, but by adopting it and perishing through it. "By an indirect method differing from that of which he so often spoke in that he himself did not understand it, Kierkegaard was an instrument for clearing the ground for a deeper conception of Christianity than that expressed by the orthodox theology, seeing that decisively and for ever he reduced certain of its dogmas to absurdity" (p. 18). This judgment must be accepted on its own merits here; as far as Kierkegaard is concerned it was based on Teisen's private opinion about his activity that it was dissolved in a jarring discord, and so must be a failure; as far as the Church was concerned it rested on the view that a religious doctrine that cannot be lived up to must be false—i.e. in both cases it was based on a humane view related to that of Koch and P. A. Rosenberg. What is of more interest in this connection is the method by which Teisen learnt that Kierkegaard's paradox theory and his conception of sin may be traced back to Athanasius and Augustine respectively; and further that these Church Fathers obtained so great an influence on Søren Kierkegaard's thought because he accepted the orthodox faith without criticism; these are the two results of Teisen's studies which are most important for our knowledge of Kierkegaard. In order to discover what relation the two conceptions bear to each other it will be convenient to recall Teisen's line of reasoning: Søren Kierkegaard accepted the orthodox tenets of faith without criticism, hence he came to rely upon Augustine and Athanasius; his religious thought therefore assumed the shape of an ellipse with the paradox and sin as the two foci. The weak link in this chain of reasoning is the assertion that Søren Kierkegaard necessarily came to rely on Augustine and Athanasius by accepting the orthodox faith; for it is a fact, which Teisen does not conceal, though it is undeniable that he tries to veil it, that Augustine's conception of sin does not enter into present-day dogmatics, which take a somewhat brighter view of humanity. "It is hardly taught any longer, not at any rate with us, that human nature is completely depraved by sin, much less—the conclusion—that God therefore must have predestined who is to be saved and who to be lost.——On the other hand it could not be prevented that Augustine's doctrine still for a long time, indeed to this very day, has cast dark shadows on religious life. However, from the errors of predestination Kierkegaard was saved by his clear thinking" (p. 71). From this it appears partly that Kierkegaard did not follow Augustine, his clear thinking preventing him, partly that Augustine's conception of sin is not orthodox, even though it still plays its pranks here and there in the rituals. Now when Teisen elsewhere in his book declares that to Søren Kierkegaard there only existed two dogmatic problems "the doctrine of human nature (sin) and the faith in the Saviour (the God man)" (56), it seems justifiable to conclude that Søren Kierkegaard neither followed Augustine nor the orthodox faith entirely, but had his own ideas about the problem of sin, and the question then arises why this was so.—That question, according to Teisen, is unwarranted, since he expressly asserts that Søren Kierkegaard refrained from independent reflections on the dogmas, which was a serious fault in him. "And here we have one of Søren Kierkegaard's essential limitations, a weakness which indeed he shares with most of his orthodox opponents, that on the whole and in the main he took up or was placed in a quite uncritical attitude towards the orthodox faith, that he, in so far as he occupied himself with systematic dogmatics altogether, in all essentials left the ortodox doctrine untouched, apparently regarding it as a matter of course that it was an unalterable expression of the tenets of the Christian faith" (p. 14). Nevertheless Teisen replied to it by showing how Kierkegaard's reaction to Hegel's philosophy, how his experience during his engagement disposed him for the inhuman theology which he later professed.—Thus there is an inner contradiction in Teisen's treatise which makes it impossible to insert the two postulates put forward there concerning Kierkegaard's relation to the tenets of the Christian faith as links in the same chain of proofs; the two cases must therefore be examined separately.

Teisen's conviction that Kierkegaard's doctrine of the paradox and of sin was due to Athanasius and Augustine respectively can hardly be said to have been reached by a scientific method; it is not based on entries in Kierkegaard's diaries, where he openly accepts the views of these Church Fathers: its correctness is indeed not proved at all but merely rendered probable. How Teisen arrived at his view does not appear from his treatise, but it must be supposed that the term "paradox" applied to Christ and the maintenance of the radical conception of sin has elicited the association Athanasius—Augustine in his mind, as these theories would presumably do in any one with a theological training. In his fuller treatment of Kierkegaard's relation to dogmatics Torsten Bohlin also cannot in any other way give grounds for his supposition that Kierkegaard is dependent on the above-mentioned early Christian theologians than the striking agreement between his and their views (cf. Torsten Bohlin, Søren Kierkegaard's Dogmatiska Åskådning, p. 216, p. 432). But the combination is no compelling necessity.

In a lecture entitled "Paganism and Christianity in Søren Kierkegaard" (delivered in the Students' Union in 1903—printed in "Udvalgte Afhandlinger" (Select Treatises) 1911, p. 124 ff.), A. B. DRACHMANN (1860-1935, classical philogist and co-editor of Søren Kierkegaard's Complete Works) with "triumphant logic" put forward the view that it was his relation to Socrates and "the Socratic" which was decisive for Kierkegaard's moulding of his belief. Drachmann maintains that the Christian definitions in "Philosophical Fragments" (the paradox—sin) were not developed from Christianity itself, but that Christianity is there built up constructively as a contrast to the humanistic view of life of which Socrates is the representative in the history of the world, and this is supposed to be the reason why the Christian dogmas of the Trinity, the Holy Ghost etc. are not included in Søren Kierkegaard's teaching. For his point of departure is the Socratic one that, viewed absolutely, all men are equal, there being only one distinction in the absolute, that between God and man. Of the most important things of existence no man can learn anything from another but only from God; if therefore a man, as Christianity demands, is to accept the teaching of Christ, then He must be God, though at the same time He is the single individual who lived in a definite historical period, i.e. Christ is the paradox. If therefore the Socratic contention about the equality of men is to be maintained in Christianity, then the doctrine, communicated by tradition from one generation to another, must be of no consequence and must cede its place to the teacher, the ideal.—Of the origin of the assumption of an absolute qualitative difference between God and man Himmelstrup expresses the following opinion, rendering possible a reconciliation between Teisen and Drachmann. "This assumption Kierkegaard may have from Socrates, to whom at any rate he refers the sharp distinction; but he may also have it from the Athanasian doctrine of the dual nature. According to this it should not be possible to solve the question concerning the paganism and Christianity of Kierkegaard, apart from the fact that the Athanasian creed of the dual nature is just such another result of reflection gained from Greek thinking (Søren Kierkegaard's Conception of Socrates" p. 247).

The second question concerning the origin of Søren Kierkegaard's dogmatic standpoint has, as we have already stated, received two contradictory answers. The official one, that Søren Kierkegaard uncritically accepted orthodoxy, is explained by the fact that his sole intention was to show the way to intensity, problems of principle therefore falling outside the scope of his mission, is a view which Teisen puts forward as a postulate but which could easily be supported by quotations from Kierkegaard's own works, e.g. the following, from the article against Dr. Rudelbach: "against the doctrine and ordering of the existing I have indeed never raised one word of objection . ." (13,477). The other, unauthorised, answer, which explains Søren Kierkegaard's special attitude to the central questions of the faith by a reference to the peculiar philosophical and personal impressions he received in his youth, the justness of which could also be proved by quotations from Kierkegaard's own writings, e.g. the following from his diary: "It is obvious that in my writings I have furnished a further definition of the concept of faith which did not exist hitherto" (E. P. 1850, p. 326), Teisen has adopted from his predecessors in Kierkegaard research, probably chiefly from Brandes.—None of these solutions of the interesting problem seem to have been the result of an actual scientific method, nor could they very well have been, seeing that there are two. It does not follow that Teisen's treatise as a whole is unmethodical, but the part dealing with Søren Kierkegaard is. For, as previously remarked, Teisen had a double purpose with his book, partly the historical one of explaining and judging the value of Søren Kierkegaard as a Christian thinker (hence the title), partly the immediate one of aiming a blow at the doctrine of the existing Church. And this furnishes a plausible explanation of the peculiar fact that one question is answered in two ways in the same work. As long as Teisen uses Kierkegaard as a means of attacking theology it is necessary to regard him as orthodox, but when he makes Kierkegaard the subject of his investigations he sees the fallacy and therefore gives a summary explanation of Kierkegaard's special attitude towards the dogmas. The priority accorded to the first explanation fully agrees with the impression received on reading Teisen's book, that it is primarily of a polemical nature.

The final result of this investigation will then be that Teisen, by studying Kierkegaard's thought against a dogmatic background, found points of contact in ecclesiastical history with the two chief doctrines in his teaching of Christianity; but Teisen's wish to have his own heretical views legalised prevented him from making this observation the starting-point of a thorough historical examination of Søren Kierkegaard's relation to theology.

5. Characterisation of the Period

The work done in the first period of Kierkegaard research only brought very modest results. The subject was outlined and the fundamental problems discussed. And this was the situation for some 40 years. No enquirers continued the work on the basis of their predecessors' results, but rewrote their books and articles. A series of closely allied subjects such as the history of Søren Kierkegaard's personal development, his relation to the orthodox doctrine, the inner coherence of the production, and the conflict with the Church, constitute the main themes which together or separately form the centre of gravity in all the treatises. Brandes, Rudin, and Chr. Jensen each gave his typical exposition of the continuity in Søren Kierkegaard's history; Brandes, Vodskov, Høffding, and Carl Koch each furnished an explanation of the psychological and dogmatic problems of the Church conflict, and so forth. They disagreed in much, but not about the cardinal points. Nor is there any doubt that whichever of these subjects you started with, if you got a good grip of it, you could pull up Søren Kierkegaard with roots and all, and ascertain how deep the roots went. And this was what was intended. A picture of Søren Kierkegaard in his full stature was wanted, a general impression. With a very few exceptions all the authors prefer an approximate understanding of the whole to a deeper insight into details.

One more feature is in common to the majority of the enquirers of the first period: none of them can conclude their works on Søren Kierkegaard without giving a general verdict on the value and significance of his activities. The universality of this latter tendency explains the above-described uniformity as regards choice of subject and planning. An evaluation of an author's contribution implies a knowledge of his intentions and his means in general; it cannot be based on an analysis of the individual works, or on studies of style or the like. Only an exposition dealing with something central in Søren Kierkegaard and thus uncovering the sources of his production or showing the hidden connection can be concluded with a judgment. Synthesis and evaluation go hand in hand.

The question then arises why they all wish to judge? P. A. Heiberg who early noted this characteristic fact gave the answer already in the preface of his first book (1895): "A number of contributions towards an account of Søren Kierkegaard as an author, a historical person, and a man, have now gradually accumulated in the literature (if Sweden and Germany are included), and a characteristic feature of them all is that their respective authors, though their works are of a scientific character, have nevertheless felt called upon in these very works, with a certain emphasis, with a certain attractive genial humour, to settle publicly their purely private account with Søren Kierkegaard. This psychological phenomenon was to me, when I read these publications, of a quite special interest, amongst other things because it seems to me to provide such an essential and such an instructive practical contribution towards the elucidation of Søren Kierkegaard's personality; Søren Kierkegaard's personality forces the objective scientific enquirer, by an arresting glance as it were, to make a subjective "preface". (Contribution to a Psychological Picture of Søren Kierkegaard, p. 2). It was this peculiarity of Søren Kierkegaard's, which was pointed out in the introduction, that caused the slow start of Søren Kierkegaard research and has made an account of it often seem to approximate to culture history. As late as the last third of the 19th century Søren Kierkegaard played a double part in Scandinavian cultural life; he was, in addition to his other aspects, the great literary genius and the great religious accuser. His critics retaliated with a similar double activity, by appearing at the same time as enquirers and judges.

This duality in the attitude of the critics manifests itself not only in the fact that their works show a certain formal uniformity by beginning with an interpretation and ending with a pronouncement of judgment. Though the last section is as a rule of small volume it frequently has considerable retrospective force. While composing the main part of their treatises the authors have been thinking of the personal appendix; their opinion of Søren Kierkegaard has set narrow limits to their understanding of him, their own humanistic or religious creed is the constantly visible foundation for their interpretation of his. Thus it is remarkable and not very likely to inspire confidence that Vodskov, Høffding, and Koch, using in the main the same method, applied to exactly the same material, arrived at three different explanations of the crisis in 1848-49, to which they yet agree to trace back the agitatorial activity in 1854-55. And to them all their solution means that just they with their special conviction and responsibility, from now on need not concern themselves with Søren Kierkegaard's accusations. But sufficient light must have been thrown on these problems. When we reviewed the individual works we showed at length for the important ones, and by some suggestions in the case of the peripherical ones, to what extent and in what forms the subjective attitude in each case came to affect the results of the investigation. Summing up we might say that in the first period it is not the knowledge of Søren Kierkegaard which increases gradually with the number of books on him, but the knowledge of what he seemed like to the representatives of the various cultural sects—with each new book the totality was revised in the light of a fresh view of life.

With P. A. Heiberg's book "Contributions towards a Psychological Picture of Søren Kierkegaard in his Boyhood and Youth" in mind, and partly also N. Teisen's "Søren Kierkegaard as a Christian Thinker", we mentioned in the preceding part that there were exceptions to the rules laid down. The two small pamphlets show plain traces of their authors' subjective attitude towards the reformer Søren Kierkegaard and thus belong to the first period; but they point beyond it—especially P. A. Heiberg, who does not attempt any evaluation of Søren Kierkegaard—by adopting narrower views than was the habit of their contemporaries; Heiberg occupies himself exclusively with the psychology of the young Kierkegaard; Teisen with the dogmatic background for his teaching of Christianity; their treatises therefore herald the future differentiation; they form two salient points in the series of publications from the first stage of Kierkegaard research which suggest its later cleavage into a psychologico-historical and a theologico-philosophical branch.

SECTION II

RESEARCH FROM 1909 TO 1949

1. THE SECOND EDITION OF THE "PAPERS"

The second edition of "Søren Kierkegaard's Papers" comprises 20 books which have been collected in 11 volumes as follows: 1 (notes from the period 1831-27/1 1837) 1909, 2 (27/1 37-2/6 40) 1910, 3 (2/6 40-20/11 42) 1911, 4 (20/11 42- /3 44) 1912, 5 (/3- /12 44) 1913, 6 (/12 44-2/12 45) 1914, 7,1-2 (2/12 45-24/1 47) 1915-16, 8,1-2 (24/1 47-15/5 48) 1917-18, 9 (15/5 48-2/1 49) 1920, 10,1-6 (2/1 49-2/11 53) 1924-34 and 11,1-3 (2/11 53-25/9 55) 1936-38-48.

The editors were P. A. HEIBERG, VICTOR KUHR, and EINER TORSTING (b. 1893), the latter being included when Heiberg's health began to give way in 1925, and he figures as co-editor from and including the 19th volume, book 2. When book 3 of the 10th volume appeared in 1927 P. A. Heiberg had died, and V. Kuhr introduced the book with a handsome obituary notice on his collaborator through many years; in it he explains "that a word like co-editor in reality gives a false impression of Heiberg's share" in the editorship; in the subordinate work as proof-reading, annotation and the like, they collaborated but the arrangement of the extensive material according to chronological and systematic principles "required control of the collective material and penetration into its smallest details, combined with a never-failing view of the totality which on this scale could in reality only be the task of one man. And as a matter of fact it can be said without the least restriction or reservation that everything that has been contributed in this field—absolutely central and decisive for the whole edition—is due to Heiberg and to him alone" (X,3, p. VIII).—At his death Heiberg left the complete manuscript of the whole work ready for the press. Its quality and systematics, which depended so much on him, are therefore constant and so his name appears as co-editor on the title-pages of all the volumes.

According to the plan the edition was to comprise all that exists in public or private ownership, or demonstrably has existed, of literary

Kierkegaard manuscripts; further documents and papers relating to Søren Kierkegaard and his family. Among the Kierkegaardian literary remains were to be counted, besides manuscripts from his own hands, also the manuscripts of others in so far as they refer to Søren Kierkegaard, and finally printed matter in which Kierkegaard had underlined some passages. According to the plan, this extensive material was to be published in three sections, first literary manuscripts with the exception of the letters, then letters from and to and concerning Søren Kierkegaard, and finally papers and documents. The edition now brought to an end only comprises the first of these sections, however, and with the limitation that, in spite of the definition, it only contains the Kierkegaard manuscripts proper. In the preface to the last book of the edition it is explained (11,3) that the original plan of publishing the documents and papers will not be adhered to because the public have not been able to augment the material to the extent which was once expected. This delays till an indefinite future not only the publication of documents, which cannot reasonably be demanded in an edition of Søren Kierkegaard's papers, but also the publication of the letters naturally belonging to this part if they have not already been published in the collected works. It is highly desirable that they should be published in a supplementary volume. For a great number of Kierkegaard's letters, especially those from his youth, with respect to their biographical and psychological value can be coordinated with the most important diary notes. Now they are scattered throughout periodicals and small books in more or less authentic versions.

As regards the reproduction of the texts it has also been necessary to make certain reservations. The main principle is reproduction in extenso and this has been applied to every text which can in any way be said to be marked by Kierkegaard's original thinking. But on the correct view that is could not be the object of the edition "to exempt the reader who was scientifically interested even in details from consulting the original manuscript" the editors have made some space-saving exceptions from the main rule. They have thus confined themselves to registering the majority of the exercise books which Søren Kierkegaard filled in a quite impersonal way during his duty work in divinity, that is to say, excerpts from lectures, translations from Greek and Hebrew and the like; further, in a number of cases they have merely stated that Kierkegaard has underlined passages in a certain book or newspaper article in the archives without quoting all these passages; and finally in the reproduction of the various drafts and fair copies for his printed works they have refrained from reproducing all the slightly varying texts and from giving a complete text-critical apparatus of variants. In this way paper for several books has been saved and the loss is slight. And in all cases where a Kierkegaardian manuscript has been omitted it has been registered in the edition with a full description.

As will appear from the introductory list of the volumes, the primary division of the material has been made on chronological principles. As in Barfod's edition, however, the chronological and systematic divisions have been combined but here with so much dexterity that one principle does not counteract the other. With support in Kierkegaard's own classification of his writings the notes have first been divided into three groups: one group having the character of diary entries (denoted A); one associated with the composition of his works (B); and one associated with his studies and reading (C). These groups are again divided into subordinate sections: thus C in æsthetics, theology, and philosophy, B in just as many sections as there are literary works begun or collected groups of notes for finished works within the period covered by the volume, and the material for group A is so divided that the notes here can be read in the same context as in the original manuscript, that is to say, that e.g. diary entries are in a group by themselves, notes on loose slips of paper by themselves, and so forth.—This far-reaching specialised division will meet the requirements of most researchers, so much the more since it has been possible to obviate in other ways that disintegration of the chronological order within the individual volumes which is its direct effect. For by providing each note within the three main sections with a serial number so that they can be easily and unambiguously designated (e.g. II B 54, where II indicates the volume, B the main section, and 54 the number within the section), the editors have provided a possibility of making a chronological index. The connected part of the A section, the registered diary notes to be found first in every volume, serve as such an index; all the dated notes within the periods covered by the respective volumes are here given in their chronological order so that the A-notes belonging there are reproduced here, and the loose A-notes and B- and C-notes are represented by their date and serial number. Since at the same time it has been attempted to carry through the chronological order within all subordinate groups a comparatively simple and effective means of approximate dating has here been provided. This excellent arrangement of the material alone makes the edition a source so easily referred to and clear that the majority of enquirers must by far prefer it to the original manuscripts.

The footnotes too contribute to this. They run as a broad stripe below the text throughout the work. They consist partly of annotations partly of cross references. The annotations are couched in the briefest possible language; they are very valuable and precise but extremely exclusive, consisting principally of historical data, biographical descriptions, references to the sources and the like, which shed light on the literary and historical background of Kierkegaard's texts, but they give no information of an instructive kind, as e.g. translations of Latin and Greek quotations, at which even a classical philologist like A. B. Drachmann made some demur. The cross references connect notes with related themes (especially A-notes) within the work: these notes are due to Heiberg alone, and the use of them shows that for once his foresight failed. Up to Volume 8 the notes are not arranged systematically, and the principle is a grouping together of notes dealing with the same literary or psychological subject. From and including Volume 8 the following information is inserted in the prefaces: "By following up and collating the cross references of the footnotes it will be possible to obtain a survey of the material for several of the most frequently occurring main ideas in the large mass of diary notes— —". At the same time the method is altered, now it is no longer the subject but words and names such as "grace", "martyrdom", "livelihood", "Luther", "Mynster", "Martensen" that constitute the elements in the web of references. Where one of these key words is mentioned, the note gives the preceding and succeeding use of it. Thus by following these references the reader can observe possible changes in the structure of Kierkegaard's ideas, and displacements in his evaluations. But if the reader wants to follow these changes through a number of years of Søren Kierkegaard's life, he must begin from the end, since references beyond the limits of the respective volumes, on account of the chronologically progressive publication, could only go back. Thus these notes may indeed afford some support, but they are awkward to use, nor are they complete. Now that the edition has been completed they should enter into a complete index volume which would save the reader much futile turning over of leaves.

Finally it should be mentioned that the editors, in addition to their unique contribution within the limits of possibility, have also tried to do the impossible, to catch the mood that emanates from the original manuscript pages. Each volume concludes with an extensive description of the manuscripts and a text-critical supplement in which amongst other things the varying size and rapidity of the hand-writing, the placing of the insertions, the dog's ears and the kind of paper used, are described. This great work must, I think, be said to have been done in vain. It is impossible to reconstruct a page of a text, far less feel its mood, by means of these commentaries.

That this new, as a whole exemplary, edition of the papers met a desideratum is shown by the extensive Kierkegaard literature which grew up simultaneously with the publication and was almost exclusively concerned with the periods in Kierkegaard's life for which the edition had supplied the material. It was a literature which, in contrast with that of the 19th century, sifted the individual problems to the bottom and dispensed with the synthesis and the judgment. The differentiation of the research was accompanied by a general striving for objectivity. Analysis and documentation replaced the approximate report and the clever summing up. A definite attitude was taken towards the material and it was handled methodically.

In accordance with the duality in Kierkegaard's activity in that he was at once a poet and a thinker, and combined in his production the individual and fictive with general reasoning, two paths have been followed in the endeavour to interpret his work: From his works enquirers have gone back to his history in order to observe ideas and motives in germ and follow their growth out of the biographical, and have thus created a psychological-historical school of research. And they have tried to understand and place Søren Kierkegaard's thought complexes and religious teaching as an element of the general culture and the cultural tradition and thus formed a philosophical-theological school of research.

2. Søren Kierkegaard as a Poet. Psychological-Historical Research

The works of the biographical Kierkegaard research fall into three main groups. The inaugurator and pioneer is P. A. Heiberg, whose books are based exclusively on the "Papers" and may almost be regarded as a "kind of expanded notes to them" (V. Kuhr: Pap. X, 3, p. XII). Later enquirers' objections to Heiberg's psychology have especially been aimed at his peculiarly boxed-in psychology, here called reflective psychology. They have justly criticised Heiberg because he considered Kierkegaard's mind an in the main isolated and unique phenomenon, the inner processes of which could be sufficiently explained by an immanent investigation, i.e. by an analysis of the entries in his diaries. And they have maintained that the essential condition for a true understanding of his life and production is that his mind is considered in a wider connection. The question as to what this connection should be has given rise to a cleavage within the psychological school of Søren Kierkegaard research, the question having been answered in two fundamentally different ways. Frithiof Brandt has tried to arrive at a deeper understanding of Kierkegaard's inner history and the genesis of his works by investigating his relation to the Copenhagen milieu in which he lived, and for that purpose has tried to procure fresh material to shed light on his external history. Hjalmar Helweg, on the other hand, has on the whole kept to the same material with which Heiberg worked, but tried to arrive at a deeper explanation of his reactions and way of thinking by considering his mind against the background of the organic milieu, the special physiological conditions under which it unfolded. Thus Heiberg's reflective psychology is resolved into two more realistic trends, one of which stresses the "social", the other the biological element. In our survey of the three groups of research works the three main figures will be subjected to a thorough analysis, while their successors or contemporaries in the same genre will only be given a brief treatment.

A. Reflective Psychology

"When one day my lover comes", Søren Kierkegaard wrote in "Viewpoint for my Work as an Author". He came in the year 1895 when the young physician P. A. Heiberg (1864-1926) instead of taking advantage of the possibilities afforded him by his medical degree, applied for a post in the Record Office in order that strenuous work might not prevent him from occupying himself with Kierkegaard. He appeared before the public for the first time with the publication of the small, important book "Contributions towards a Psychological Picture of Søren Kierkegaard in his Boyhood and Youth" (1895 cf. above p. 42 ff), and showed his faithfulness by working with Kierkegaard as editor and interpreter till his death. At that juncture research on Søren Kierkegaard's papers had changed its appearance under his hands, and his own mind and his language had assumed its colouring from the master. An assimilation process of a rarely intimate kind had taken place. We only know the last stages of its consummation. In the little book of 1895 Heiberg appears as a young academic, happy in his love of Søren Kierkegaard and eagerly occupied with the thoughts and books of the time. When he again came forward with his opinions as an author his development was at an end, his physiognomy as a scholar had acquired its lasting character of dry passionateness. His mind had closed round Søren Kierkegaard, and he had developed into a crank among men, and an exception among writers.

The complete familiarity with Søren Kierkegaard's reading and thoughts, with his habits, handwriting, and punctuation, which Heiberg achieved during these thirty-odd years of penetrative study has been of incalculable value for the new edition of Søren Kierkegaard's papers. But on the other hand, his one-sided reading and his local omniscience, which made him an excellent editor and commentator, impaired his research work. His original works on Søren Kierkegaard are indeed distinguished by a rare ingenuity and surpassing constructive imagination, but in their method they are so deeply marked by his one-sidedness, by his lack of knowledge of æsthetic rules and literary conventions, that one will often doubt the scientific value of his results. It has been maintained about Heiberg's Kierkegaard studies that they "grew steadily in pertinence and congeniality with their subject, culminating finally in the truly 'psychological microscopy' of the main work." The contention is true in so far as his last book actually is better and more reliable than the previous works, but this is not because Heiberg himself underwent a development but because the material for his last book is of quite another kind than that of the former ones. When Søren Kierkegaard's youthful æsthetisising years were over and he had come to the end of his work as a pseudonymous author, he changed his literary tactics, not only officially, but his notes ad se ipsum also in a remarkable degree changed character from the indirect literary to the downright self-reflecting kind. The enquirer into Kierkegaard's personal development after 1845 will therefore only be exposed to a limited number of the pitfalls and snares lying in wait for the author dealing with the young enigmatical and heavily burdened Søren Kierkegaard in the decade between 1835 and 1845, he will not fail a prey to premonitions or find an opportunity of propounding a fraction of the hypotheses which so to speak gratuitously present themselves to the reader of Søren Kierkegaard's early diaries. That it is to this we must ascribe Heiberg's greater pertinence in his last book, and not to the increase with years of his level-headedness and shrewdness, appears amongst other things from the fact that he remained faithful to the most daring constructions of the "Episode" and the "Segment".

These books, "En Episode i Søren Kierkegaards Liv" (An Episode in S. K.'s Life, 1912), "Et Segment af Søren Kierkegaards religiøse Udvikling" (A Segment of Søren Kierkegaard's Religious Development, 1918), and "Søren Kierkegaards religiøse Udvikling. Psykologisk Mikroskopi". (Søren Kierkegaard's Religious Development, Psychological Microscopy, 1925) must not, incidentally, be regarded as separate books but as parts of a large connected work, the object of which is to elucidate Søren Kierkegaard's religious development from July 1835 to June 1852, i.e. from the time when he first tried to become clear as to his view of life and set it forth in writing, until 17 years later he overcame all questions of doubt and achieved faith in the deepest sense. In the sequel this peculiar and unique work will now be reviewed and criticised. Diffuseness will be necessary here more than elsewhere because Heiberg is, and is generally regarded as, the pioneer in Scandinavian Kierkegaard research, and as a result has exerted great influence on literally all later enquirers.

The first little book on the "Episode" forms the introduction to the work. It tells us nothing about Søren Kierkegaard's spiritual development but supplies material for a deeper understanding of it by informing us of a hitherto unknown event which with "a probability bordering on certainty" can be inserted in Søren Kierkegaard's youthful life. The following episode is said to have taken place: "In the year 1836, perhaps especially in the months March to May, Søren Kierkegaard had a regular period of dissipation: restaurant life with plenty of drinking even to the point of intoxication, visits to the theatre and to other pleasure haunts with casual, more or less frivolous restaurant acquaintances, where Søren Kierkegaard gave the "joking devil" free play. A particularly wild bacchanal, though be it noted, not in female society, but evidently with a most extravagant æsthetic equipment, food and drink, during which a sophisticated perhaps also cynical, specificially masculine, verve in speech and enjoyment prevailed, ended so far as Søren Kierkegaard was concerned in so heavy an intoxication that he became almost quite unconscious. The day after this debauch he woke up with a feeling that the premonition and fear already long harboured that this racket must end disastrously, had now at last come true—now it was to come to an end. He broke off all communication with his boon companions. Several months after this bacchanal we see that suddenly, "with a tremendous force and urge to be heard", there cropped up in Kierkegaard's mind a recollection of a sequel, the recollection that while in his almost totally unconscious state of intoxication he was taken by his boon companions to "one of those places where curiously enough you pay money for a woman's despicability." What happened there he does not know but with the sudden recollection the idea of what may possibly have happened strikes him like lightning."

This summary of the "Episode" forms the introduction to the next book the "Segment", the starting point of which is Kierkegaard's situation immediately after the lapse in the spring of 1836. It is true that Søren Kierkegaard's religious development in the whole period from the 1st of June 1835 to the 19th of May 1838 is treated in the "Segment", but since the understanding of how Søren Kierkegaard could enter upon the downward road of profligacy implies a knowledge of the notes he made in his diary from October 1836 to February 1837, Heiberg, for practical reasons, broke the chronological line. In the account to follow, which in the main can only give the results, not the arguments, the exposition follows the actual sequence of events.

In the course of the first two summer months in 1835 Søren Kierkegaard conquered his former scepticism and Faustian unrest and achieved a state of happy resolution which found its eloquent expression in a long entry in the diary, dated Gilleleje, August 1. Here he expressed his will now to find the idea for which he could live and die; it was to happen through self-knowledge and action, not through futile brooding—and no obstacle should be capable of stopping him in his endeavours. After a few days he returned to Copenhagen to begin putting his plans into execution. They consisted amongst other things in his preparing for graduation in divinity. It was then that the so-called earthquake took place. For a number of years Søren Kierkegaard's old father had, as it were drop by drop, instilled anxious misgivings into his mind by obscure allusions to or actual sudden attacks of a melancholy which he kept hidden in daily life. Now when Kierkegaard returned home ready for a great display of energy on an unusual scale he was abruptly checked in his rising course—presumably in August and September—on witnessing that his father was seized with the most severe attacks of melancholy. He divined that this melancholy had its root in some iniquity committed by his father and that the divine wrath rested on him and his whole family; its head, the old man, would survive his children and thus "remain, a cross on the tomb of his own hopes". The effect of these terrible discoveries was that Søren Kierkegaard withdrew from his father, Christianity became a stumbling block to him, and in melancholy desperation he caught at "the intellectual side of man" alone. In the time that followed he occupied himself mainly with æsthetic and romantic topics, amongst others the legendary figures of Don Juan, Faustus, and Ahasuerus, he had no thought of preparing for a degree; divinity was now only the subject of philosophical reflections, and he noted the irreconcilability of philosophy and Christianity. As a further reaction against the sad perspectives for his future adumbrated by the earthquake, he gave himself up to a life of dissipation and reckless expenditure at restaurants. He drank, contracted debts, and in May his misery came to a head when a merry evening terminated in a brothel. Søren Kierkegaard's mental state in the ensuing summer was not marked by any sense of sin, intellectualism dominates his notes. Some time in the autumn he became acquainted with Hamann's writings; they seem to cause a stir in the suppressed religious stratum of his mind, and he heaved a sigh in his yearning for his life's dissonance to be resolved in harmony. But his standpoint seems unchanged; for the summer and autumn it may be described by the term resignation. On the 8th of October a recollection of the events on that appalling evening suddenly cropped up, and the religious undercurrent rose to the surface in a deep and sudden sense of sin. On that day his religious development began: it is true that we cannot in the notes from the following months trace any disintegration of the purely intellectual strata of his mind, but in the time after the awakening of the recollection Søren Kierkegaard is seen to seek a psychological explanation of the origin of sin in the individual, which finds expression in his occupation with the medieval notions of the kingdom of evil and the fatal power evil may gain over a man, and with the Karpocratian doctrine that the way to perfection can be reached by making a trial of all the vices. An occupation which Vigilius Haufniensis, whose book "The Concept of Dread" has proved to be closely connected with the critical period in Søren Kierkegaard's youth, thinks he can interpret as a manifestation of fear gazing at guilt with an ambiguous mixture of sympathy and antipathy.—The diaries from the beginning of 1837 seem to testify that Søren Kierkegaard had then fully realised the fact of the earthquake in his father's life, the fact which in 1847 he describes in the entry quoted hundreds of times: "The terrible event with the man who, once when he was a small boy tending sheep on the Jutland heath, suffering great hardships, and benumbed with cold, on a hill stood up and cursed God—and that man was unable to forget it when he was 82 years old."—And this knowledge had a double effect: confirmation of his suspicion had a soothing effect on him and thus rendered possible an objective consideration of the events that had taken place, by which he discovered the connection between his own and his father's guilt; the fear which his father's fits of melancholy left in him, the sinister thoughts of sin and the wrath of God drove him to aberrations; for fear, he now thinks, is the effect of original sin on the individual. In March and April Søren Kierkegaard's world of concepts and his ideas are stirred, and we can observe that in his mind the stress is being transferred from the sphere of cognition to the sphere of emotion; previously he felt like a Faustus, a sceptic, now like an Ahasuerus, a despairing man. And finally in the days around the 1st of May the awakening to Christianity takes place which was heralded by the recording of his recollection of the 8th of October 1836. He decides upon conversion and a public confession of his sins, he means to "wander the same way back as he has advanced, while the consciousness that his sins have been forgiven keeps him up, encourages him, and prevents despair—like one who fully sensible of his sin denounces himself and now cheerfully goes to meet even the death of the evil-doers—". Under the influence of his morbid melancholy Kierkegaard regarded himself as an evil-doer, not as a sinner, which involved that he condemned himself to a sad, life-long penitence. His healthy nature protested, he abandoned his purpose and turned again to the world to rule there for some time yet. Then he was overtaken by God and brought to a state of complete contrition; the first person that met him on his way from the monastic cell, was a quite young innocent girl (Regine) for whom he immediately conceived a violent passion which again—immediately—inspired the idea that by his visit to the brothel, which in these very days lived in his memory, he had not only lost his purity but had perhaps also become the father of a child; the thought of a public confession and all the misery which this would bring down on him, overwhelmed him again: "Everybody will now despise me, oh my God, do not abandon me,—let me live and improve—". The entries from the ensuing time again show a reaction; impersonal reflections on æsthetic and philosophic subjects fill the diaries, he ponders on a future career as an author; in respect of the Christian avowal of sin he gets into a chronic critical state; on the one hand he wants definitively to be converted, on the other hand, conversion has by his melancholy been made identical with a life-long penitence and a confession humiliating to man. His soul shrank from this radical Christian cure until at last it lost all its flexibility and in the last months of the year a complete faintness, a deadly apathy seized upon him. The first three months of the new year are almost devoid of entries in the diaries, in the few that are found Kierkegaard shows a ghastly death's head grin, in March he is silent like a closed grave, overcome by a quiet despair. On the 1st of April he declares, "I will now try to make an effort again. Poul Møller has died." It was presumably the news of Poul Møller's death which roused Kierkegaard to the present again. His efforts resulted in some notes marked by quiet sadness and resignation; he occupies himself with his personal relation to the faith, but thinks (April 22) that if Christ is to dwell in him he must come in through closed doors, that is to say, God must open them, he cannot do so himself. "And God sends the powerful word. On May 19, at 10.30 a.m. Søren Kierkegaard testifies to it in his diary: "There is an unspeakable joy which, as it were, thrills us inexplicably, appears without motive like the cry of the apostle: rejoice, and again I say: rejoice.—Not a joy because of this or that but the cry of the full soul "with tongue and mouth, and from the depths of the heart": I rejoice at my joy, of, in, with, at, on, by and with my joy—which, as it were, cuts off the rest of our song: a joy which like a breeze cools and refreshes, a blast from an Etesian gale blowing from the plain of Mamre to eternal abodes.—"Here is more than fairy-story and music. For the first time Søren Kierkegaard felt what after 10 years he expressed in these words: the happy side of my life, this hitherto, God be praised, inexhaustible and for ever rejuvenated source of joy: that God is love."

In his last monumental work Heiberg deals chiefly with Kierkegaard's notes from 1847 to 1852; it does not, however, unjustly bear the general title "Søren Kierkegaard's Religious Development"; the whole movement from the "Earthquake" to the last awakening is described in it, only the extreme crises and lengthy deliberations of the last years at greater length. The book begins with the quotation of a note from June 1852 in which Søren Kierkegaard expresses his decision to abide by his resolution of basing his financial existence on the continued use of the remainder of his capital, without trying to safeguard himself as regards his living, thus to persevere as long as there is merely the slightest possibility, and it concludes with the following summing up by Heiberg: "— —to me the change that has taken place in the content of the concept of "dissimilarity" in Søren Kierkegaard's mind compared with the content as defined in the year 1835 and as late as the year 1848 illuminates—as by a flash of lightning—what is central in the whole religious development of Søren Kierkegaard, as a development from a piety morbidly coloured by melancholy to a healthy religiousness which by its intense vivid existential relation to the demand: to arrive at sobriety by dying from this world, is decisively coloured by Christianity, is coloured by something which, it is true, has all the existentially Christian criterion: quid nimis, but this has nothing to do with melancholy.—This result quite agrees with Kierkegaard's own: from innate fear to faith. Viewed thus the whole thing may be summed up in one word: the history of his "recovery".—It appears from this passage that the gist of Heiberg's exposition of Søren Kierkegaard's religious development is the explanation of the changes in the period from the autumn of 1835 to the summer of 1852 which took place in Kierkegaard's notion of dissimilarity, his dissimilarity from the ordinary man; in what follows, therefore, the line of development taken by this notion will be traced, while the unravelling of the many related dialectical problems will as far as possible be disregarded.

Søren Kierkegaard's notion of being an exception goes far back in his history and has been determining for the course and issue of all the crises in his life; it is at first reflected especially in his thoughts about his melancholy, later also in his reflections on his financial situation and his possibility of applying for a benefice. This idea of being an exception developed in the 22-year-old Kierkegaard as a result of the "Earthquake" in the autumn of 1835. In its first form it was quite negative, connected with Old Testament ideas of God and formed by a melancholy imagination. In his wrath at Michael Kierkegaard's sins God was thought to have deprived his descendants in the first generation of every possibility of temporal happiness and to have destined them for an early death. In the months April-May 1837, when Søren Kierkegaard seriously began to understand the extent of his own guilt, the idea of exceptionality received a bitter accretion; he regards himself as an evil-doer who indeed can be given a share of God's grace but all his days must suffer punishment in the form of melancholy and do penance for his sin. These imperative ideas were not altered when in May 1838 Søren Kierkegaard experienced the religious awakening which gave him the unshakable belief that God is love, but it strengthened his belief in the forgiveness of sins. Not until 1841 did the idea of exceptionality receive a positive contribution when he became aware that by undergoing the sufferings attaching to the exceptional position of melancholy he was led to make discoveries which might benefit others; the background of this change was that awakening of his creative genius which took place simultaneously with the crisis of his engagement[1]. The pseudonymous works were written on the dual view that his dissimilarity to the ordinary run of men can be traced back in an æsthetic objective respect to his genius while in a subjective religious respect it must be regarded as a result of his melancholy, which again is a punishment for sin; the series terminated in 1846 with "Unscientific Postscript", and it was Kierkegaard's intention to let this work conclude the whole production. He now meant to retire to a small living in the country to perform the duty of doing penance with which he had tormented himself since 1837. But when his purpose was to be put into practice it proved to be connected with almost insoluble problems; if he came out of his isolation and tried to get into contact with the world in general, would not that entail a duty to break his silence (i.e. to make a public confession of the interaction between father and son, of their melancholy and their sins)? And this confession, which in a worldly sense was humiliating, was perhaps not even permissible in a religious sense, might perhaps be interpreted as an attempt to play providence. Meditations on these questions came to an end without any decision in June 1846, when Søren Kierkegaard's urge to produce broke out—in consequence of the persecution in the Corsair and the events centring round Adler—and in practice it conquered the idea of penance which, however, still remained as a theoretical consideration in his mind; thus he kept on writing and could do so without feeling at variance with his religious duty, for the situation had now changed. On the one hand his position as an author had become intolerable since the Corsair's onslaught upon him, and on the other hand, the religious confusion prevalent in the capital was gradually becoming extreme; a guide was needed, that is to say, by continuing his work as an author and staying in town he would satisfy his self-tormenting inclinations, and at the same time he might perhaps, as the only man in all the country, clear up the religious confusion. Søren Kierkegaard now regarded himself as an "extraordinary" person who had a special divine mission, and his position as the sum

1. In "Nogle Bidrag til Enten-Eller's Tilblivelseshistorie" (Some Contributions to the History of the Origin of Either-Or; Studier fra Sprog- og Oldtidsforskning, vol. XX, part 3) P. A. Heiberg has furnished a probable proof that Assessor Vilhelm's treatise on "The æsthetic Validity of Marriage" was written already in the engagement period and that it was a fruit of "the painful deliberations of Kierkegaard's conscience, Dare you get engaged, dare you marry".

of doing penance and doing good; he had thus arrived at a teleological view of his melancholy.

This was the situation when Søren Kierkegaard in May 1847 began to take up his melancholy for renewed examination; he bethought himself that he ought perhaps to try to remove this thorn in the flesh, by which he would become happier in a final sense and might be able to take a living, but after all he thought it best to refrain and remain in his position as an "extraordinary" person in the service of the idea; that the idea of pulling out the thorn in his flesh and becoming a parson was here dismissed and a writer's profession chosen for religious reasons, was due to the fact that the idea of a living was not now connected with the notion of doing penance, but with his wish to improve or safeguard his more and more precarious financial position. He himself called his resolve a decision of infinity, the expression implying that his standpoint at this time may be regarded as identical with religiousness A, the view of life implying infinite resignation. In the late summer of the same year the idea of getting rid of his melancholy was again taken up for consideration but then the affection was again viewed in relation to the idea of penance; he now meant to try to get rid of his melancholy by joining the thought of his melancholy to that of God, by trying to forget the guilt which God in his mercy had forgiven, and these endeavours testify that Kierkegaard was now approaching the specifically Christian stage, religiousness B. For A is marked among other features by the eternal preservation of sin in the memory, B by the full forgiveness, by the paradoxical belief that everything is possible to God, i.e. not only to forgive but also to forget the sin. In the time that follows the diaries are silent about the continuation of this line of development and his struggle against his melancholy; not until the 18th of April did it find expression in an entry, but then, indeed, with extreme intensity: "My whole nature is changed. My secretiveness and reticence are broken—I must speak. Great God, give grace." Further on in the entry he expresses his belief that Christ will now help him to remove his melancholy; however, this sudden change merely heralds a long and exhausting crisis; already on April 24 he gave up the thought of speaking, at any rate now, and reverted to the idea of penance, of having to bear the pain and penalty throughout his life. Even though the sudden religious revival did not acquire the epoch-making significance that Søren Kierkegaard expected at the moment he experienced it, it did not after all remain without effect; the idea, so far abstract and passive, of the terrible sufferings and anguish of his melancholy was now rendered concrete and resolved into three active ideas, (1) his reticence, (2) the recollection of guilt, and (3) the possibility that his melancholy under cover of his reticence might become a cause for him to despair that God would be able to help him temporally; the latter idea of despair is new and must be associated with the thoughts simultaneously given form by Kierkegaard in the paper "The Sickness unto Death", where despair is declared to be a sin.—Finally on May 11 the crisis came to an end with the result that Kierkegaard realised that so far his religious stage had been resignation, which is a form of despair, and that he was now confronted by the choice of faith in the deepest sense: the conviction that to God everything is possible, and the state in which the ego is grounded transparently in the power that constituted it. This state of faith, which is described in the "Sickness unto Death", is equal to the rebirth, i.e. the second birth to death to the world, after the first birth into the world in worldliness, a repetition of immediacy in a sphere of a higher quality, which is attained when resignation has been intensified to death to the world in a Christian sense, so that the old immediacy has been killed, the vital nerve in the individual's relation to the world cut through. But where the path turns off from resignation to death to the world in a Christian, absolute sense, there Kierkegaard was stopped by his melancholy, which led him away from absorption in himself to external reflections and polemics against the world around him. In October-November 1848, he got over the dead point and finally, after 11 years' anxieties and struggles, gave up "the point which a melancholy, morbid reflection made to him the firmest in his arbitrariness and wilfulness; the conception of the painful recollection inspired by his idea of penance" (228). In the deepest sense he seized upon the idea "to God everything is possible"; his approach to the Christian standpoint terminated, he had reached religiousness B. But as Søren Kierkegaard proceeded on his way and tried to become clear as to what his own mission as a believer was, "he comes to the next (and last) milestone: Christ as the prototype with the claim that he should be imitated", and an intermission crisis was again imminent. The ideal question as to whether he should strive after martyrdom or remain a poet obtruded itself upon him in the shape of the actual problem whether he should publish the three papers "The Sickness unto Death", "Viewpoint for my Work as an Author", and "Training in Christianity", and if so, in what way. If he let the last two, in which the demands made on the Christian were pushed to extremity and the existing form of Christianity was denounced, appear under his own name, he would run the risk of being killed for the sake of truth, like a martyr. The first half of the year 1849 passed in interminable reflections; his melancholy urged him in the direction of imitation, a host of objections restrained him; at the end of June he realised his position; the two polemical pamphlets against the Church were published pseudonymously by Anti-Climacus; this emphasised that Søren Kierkegaard did not judge but was himself subject to judgment in the pamphlets. He was now no longer brought to a standstill before Christ as the prototype, but found rest in the belief that the death of Christ was the expiation. With this, melancholy had finally been conquered, its power over Kierkegaard was broken.

There now only remained one undecided question, how the boundaries of the domain that could be left to the poetical part of him could be determined, how far he could venture as a poet so as to lend existential support to the idea of his cause. The question was related to that of his getting a living which was now of more immediate interest than ever, seeing that his capital had shrunk so much that it was necessary for him to think of earning his living by work. The first phase of this struggle with his thoughts came to an end in July-August 1850: Kierkegaard temporarily arrived at an understanding of the ideal significance it might have for his cause if he refrained from becoming a clergyman and endured the pain, continuing to spend the rest of his fortune. He made no final decision in the matter but kept it in abeyance in the succeeding months, waiting for a decree from above to solve the dilemma whether he should proceed in the direction of keeping to the "dissimilarity" or in the direction of humanity in general and secure a competence by obtaining a clerical office. Then in March 1851 Bishop Mynster published his "Further Contributions to the Deliberations on the Conditions of the Church in Denmark", which offended Søren Kierkegaard because he was there called an intelligent author while his tormentor Goldschmidt was called a talented author, and this insult from the bishop made Kierkegaard further aware of his isolated position in relation to the existing Church. He decided definitely to give up applying for a clerical office. On the 19th of July 1852 his deliberations, which had lasted for years, as to realising the common lot were terminated by the resolve not to apply for any office at all but to continue to spend his capital. And now he understood his mission as follows: "The imitation (of Christ) must be introduced. But without „authority", this is and remains my category. And this has indeed happened, for in "Of my Work as an Author" and in the preface to "Two Discourses at the Communion" and later on by self-examination I have declared myself to be a poet. For "Grace" is the crucial thing, but imitation must be introduced, but neither I nor others will be made anxious beyond our powers, therefore I am only "a poet"; however, my life has already long expressed more than being a poet, and will express more if I remain in "dissimilarity"" (p. 374).

Heiberg's investigation is a product of the unique psychological material, in the form of 21 years' carefully kept diaries, which Kierkegaard left at his death. The psychological knowledge he wished to gain from this material was, more precisely defined, Søren Kierkegaard's religious development, as will indeed appear from the above surveys and from the titles of his last two books. The subtitle of the last, "Psychological Microscopy", indicates an important feature of his method: that the elements of the investigation are minimal quantities, some few periods of the diaries, sentences from these; but only when the concept of microscopy is joined to the concept of development does it become clear that the aim of the work is to demonstrate the family aspect and the individuality aspect of the various entries, that is to say, establish under which aspect the detail is to be viewed so as to segregate that by which it is unique, an idea, or thought, or merely the foreshadowing of a future thought. In all its boldness the idea then is to reconstruct Kierkegaard's thought complexes and the changes in their structure. It follows that the maximum scope of Heiberg's investigation lies within the limits bounding the manifest content of Søren Kierkegaard's mind. Heiberg regarded this delimitation of his field of work as a matter of course: "In so far as it is really Kierkegaard's mind which is the interest and subject of our understanding", the object is precisely to take care "not to go outside the sphere of reflection which is limited by Søren Kierkegaard's mind" (Rel. Udv. p. 7). According to Heiberg, then, the psychic processes, the course of which could be followed in fragments in the diaries, could be exhaustively described in respect to their origin and growth if you knew the complete content of Kierkegaard's consciousness; and without arguing he assumes that the parts of Kierkegaard's mind that have been preserved in the papers are sufficient for a reconstruction of the principal patterns of his moods and thoughts; his psychology therefore has a literary character,—in contrast with all other modern psychology which seeks support in biology, the doctrine of types, and theories of the subconscious and unconscious zones of the mind—it is a purely reflective psychology; and it is based on the assumption, probably incapable of proof, of the value of the material.

If we accept the psychological theory and the assumption of the sufficiency of the material, there still remains a problem, however. The object is to demonstrate coherence, more precisely defined as development, i.e. continuity; but in the psychological sphere continuity is a doubtful category. Even if we start from the principle that psychic elements are connected by a causative relation this can hardly be proved. For it is necessary for the enquirer to acquaint himself with larger or smaller portions of the accessible material and on the basis hereof propound a theory of the nature of the development. If the material he is dealing with is rich and of many shades he will run the risk of being able to cover the lines of his hypothesis with quotations which show a striking agreement with his anticipations, though these do not accord with the facts; his results and contentions may be documented at such length that apparently there can be no doubt as to their correctness, and yet merely be an echo of his method. The only way in which the justice of such an objection can be proved is to demonstrate that the method in the concrete case has led to doubtful or downright untrustworthy results, that the hypothesis has involved or necessitated a forced, factitious, or quite impossible interpretation of the individual texts which constitute the elements of the exposition. In the sequel we shall therefore examine Heiberg's analyses; our examination will fall into two divisions, the first of which deals with Heiberg's use and understanding of the downright personal notes, and the second with his interpretations of the æsthetic notes and writings which for one reason or another must be supposed to bear a particularly intimate relation to Kierkegaard's person, though this is not revealed by the form.

An enquirer so scrupulous and so zealous for truth as Heiberg will not of course be able quite to disregard phenomena which seem to militate against his hypotheses; but when he comes across such refractory entries, for instance containing material for thought long since used up and rejected, or when he is hampered by a troublesome lack of information on some supposed change of view or other, he makes use of a strange practice which may inspire confidence at the moment. He does not indeed abandon the conjecture he has once put forward, but he inserts what might be called an epicycle, i.e. an extra hypothesis according to which the actual movement is checked or obscured by a feebler movement in the opposite direction. A characteristic example of a forced interpretation as well as of the ensuing formation of an epicycle is afforded by his analysis of the famous entry of October 8, 1836. "It is very strange, the queer way, in which something that has passed long ago may suddenly come into one's mind, for instance the recollection of something wrong, of which one has hardly been aware at the moment of action—flashes of lightning indicating a great storm. They do not step forward, but properly speaking leap forward with an enormous strength and urgency to be heard. Thus on the whole, I suppose that passage in the Gospel must be understood that on the day of judgment men shall give account of every idle word they have spoken" (I.A. 254—the most important entry for Heiberg's "Episode" and "Segment"). What Heiberg makes of this note will appear from the above account. It is the one that connects the May entry about inebriate, dissolute living with the bookkeeper's history and thus lays the foundation for the hypothesis about the Episode in Søren Kierkegaard's youthful life —an insecure foundation, for what the note contains of destiny Heiberg himself, I think, must be said to have read into it. There is nothing to justify the assumption that the recollection refers to grave immorality during drunkenness; on the contrary, the quiet words: "something wrong one was not aware of at the moment of action", exclude such an interpretation; the note must have been made under the pressure of misgivings. Brix's commentary on it seems obviously right: "It is concerned with behaviour whose character during the action you have not time or a sufficiently clear view to judge of at the moment. When it crops up later on, you say: "Really, that was a characteristically nasty remark of mine" (Analyses and Problems III, p. 289). The last part of the note now gives Heiberg a chance—with how much right we shall discuss in another connection—to note an outcropping of the suppressed religious stratum in Søren Kierkegaard's mind, in that he comes into contact with the consciousness of sin in a Christian sense. It might be expected that the criterion for the correctness of this interpretation would be that the Christian awakening had left its traces in the diaries in the ensuing period. But this it has not done. Heiberg says: "But that, nevertheless, here again, in spite of the violent effect which gave Søren Kierkegaard a presentiment of "a great storm", we have a right to characterise the religious revival as merely momentary, is shown by the circumstance that the whole year the purely intellectual strata of the mind, apparently quite undisturbed, keep the ascendancy, not to say the absolute power in Kierkegaard's thoughts, in so far as we are enabled to follow them through the notes" (The "Segment" p. 35). The circumstances which definitely render impossible the already daring conjecture, are explained away, or are adduced as a proof of the correctness of Heiberg's opinion that the religious revival was momentary, an opinion which he can only have expressed in the preceding part because he knew what was coming. In life it is an art to reduce your anticipations so much that reality surpasses them, but in research it is suspect.—In a quite similar manner Heiberg in Rel. Udv. reduces the importance of a note which weightily seems to contradict a hypothesis just mentioned; Heiberg contrived to render probable that Kierkegaard in the period from August 16, 47 to the autumn of 48 carried to a triumphant end his offensive against his melancholy thought (that his youthful sin was forgiven him but for the rest of his life he was to remember his guilt and do penance), that he had even come to feel so sure of his standpoint in relation to the right Christian view of the forgiveness of sins and the atonement that he could even go against "a conception in "Handbuch deutscher Beredsamkeit" which is exactly like that to which his idea of penance so far has so obstinately kept him tied" (Rel. Udv. p. 186). And yet Heiberg thinks, to the surprise of the reader, that we should not believe so firmly in his victory. He has a somewhat obscure suspicion "that this victory, in the theoretical as well as the practical, has not yet in a quite similar manner been represented by Kierkegaard's ultimate liberation from the power of the idea of penance in the theoretical field" (p. 187). It is not clear whence Heiberg has derived his suspicion if it is not from the note which with good reason he believes will substantiate the justice of his suspicion: "As a man I am personally in more than the common sense a sinner who has been far enough on the road to perdition, whose conversion only too often was marked and is marked by lapses—a sinner who yet believes that all that sin is forgiven him for Christ's sake, even though he must bear the consequence of the punishment; a sinner who longs for eternity to thank Him and His love" (p. 187-IX A, 189). These lines, which date from July-August 1848, point back to a stage in Kierkegaard's development from the time before "The Sickness unto Death", preceding, too, all the impulses approximating to a belief in the importance of atonement for this life. By the insertion of an epicycle, the view that Søren Kierkegaard, though he had indeed practically and theoretically conquered the idea of doing penance, had not finally shaken it off theoretically (?), the contradictory views are reconciled in a but little convincing way. It is the same procedure as is adopted at general meetings when a fractious member is given a seat on the board of directors.—Such obscuring epicycles occur again and again in Heiberg's two large volumes. As will appear clearly from the first example, they are based on the cleavage of Kierkegaard's mind into various strata independent of each other; an æsthetic objective as against a subjective religious stratum, a practical as against a theoretical, a sound as against a morbid stratum etc., which is consistently carried through both in the Segment and Rel. Udv. This stratification which in itself may be termed an epicycle, makes it possible partly to render innocuous the various notes which do not agree with the general exposition by referring them to those spheres of Kierkegaard's mind which are most remote from his inmost personal self. In this way their effect is reduced: they do not bring about any break in the demonstrated continuity, but merely a pause in the development, a delaying distraction.

As a transition to the investigation of Heiberg's procedure in the case of the literary and æsthetic documents which for some reason or other are thought to be personally connected with Kierkegaard, we may mention his use of the metaphors and similes occurring in the diaries. The entry dated October 8th 1836 may again serve as a point of departure. Its last lines following immediately after he has mentioned the sudden humiliating recollection run as follows: "Thus, on the whole, I suppose, that passage in the Gospel must be understood that on the day of judgment men shall give account of every idle word they have spoken." Heiberg thinks they express "the sudden impulse seriously to take upon himself as guilt not only the brutish state of drunkenness after that bacchanal but the very things he may have committed in such a state. This impulse, the realisation of which at the time when he writes down his experiences can only be regarded as an anticipation, interests him with a certain exegetic detachment, as an illustration of the enormous stringency of the demand for self-consciousness and consciousness of guilt implied in the words of the Gospel that men have to account for every idle word on the day of judgment. In other words, in this note we have— — — plainly enough a manifestation of what we have called the second, the subjective, ethical current in Søren Kierkegaard's relation to religion, especially the Christian religion" (Segment p. 35). And a couple of pages further on Heiberg says: "Let us now pause a moment at the relatively important element in Kierkegaard's religious development when he, though transiently, yet under a fairly deep subjective impression comes into contact with the Christian concept of sin— — —" (p. 37). How utterly absurd such an interpretation is would not have escaped Heiberg's own attention if he had tried to turn his analytical practice in the concrete case into a general proposition, an æsthetic doctrine; this would imply that knowledge of the sphere from which a writer derives his similes also affords knowledge of his view of life or moral aspiration at the time of writing, and that the second term of a comparison should serve to enlighten one about the consequence of the state described in the first. It is unnecessary to argue against such a theory. Of course it is right that the similes used by a poet give much information about him, but not about his faith or moral aspirations, but about his interests and knowledge and about his mood. In this connection we must also refer to the general opinion about metaphors, that their object is not to define intellectually, but to fire the imagination. In the case in point the enquirer would not, therefore, justly be able to draw any other psychological conclusion than this: the author of the notes had exegetical interests, which is indeed confirmed by the facts. Similar though not quite identical examples of a disregard of observed fundamental traits of the poetic metaphorical language may be met with amongst other things in the analysis of the notes on the Earthquake, the Evil-doer, and the Joking Devil (Segment pp. 73-74, 150-52,158).

It may seem unjust to counter Heiberg's theory with æsthetic theories, when he expressly declares that Søren Kierkegaard's mind is the sole interest and object of his work, but the fact is that an interpretation of an author's mentality in literary matters must invariably be misleading if no account is taken of the circumstance that the documents used are literature, and therefore must only be explained psychologically if they cannot be explained æsthetically. And neither in his treatment of Kierkegaard's half lyrical notes from his youth nor of his actual poetical production has Heiberg taken account of this, so that a literary criticism of his work must be considered justifiable.

Those parts of Kierkegaard's production with which Heiberg's method of examination has played such havoc that they seem to have given false witness are numerous. As examples may be mentioned the paper about Johannes Climacus ("Søren Kierkegaard in Boyhood and Youth"), the description of a case of collision in "The Concept of Dread" (Segment p. 6), several of the study notes on medieval literature, presentiments, and fear (Segment pp. 33-50), the lecture "He is believed in the world" (Rel. Udv. pp. 83-86), but above all the inserted pieces in "Guilty—Not Guilty", which from the first days of Kierkegaard research have enjoyed an undeserved reputation as autobiographical sources and records for information about the Kierkegaard family's presumed dissolute erotic life. A critical examination of Heiberg's interpretation of the bookkeeper's history (Episode pp. 17-54) must here serve as an example of them all. The novel deals with a bookkeeper who on a picnic with depraved friends drinks till he is quite fuddled and in a semi-conscious state is taken by them to a brothel. Long afterwards the recollection of the event crops up in his memory and gives him the fixed idea that perhaps he is the father of a child. This idea makes him a lonely crank, it worries and persecutes him till he is almost crazy, for as his friends have gone to America it is impossible for him to learn whether his presentiment is true. On his deathbed he at last gets rid of the dreaded possibility, "it was a delusion". This story Heiberg introduces into Søren Kierkegaard's life as a termination to his period of dissipation in 1836, and he finds the justification for it in the following facts: at an older age Kierkegaard mentions that in his youth he had wandered on the road to perdition, had been guilty of excesses and gone astray; the inserted pieces all seem to contain an autobiographical element; and some rather irrelevant conversations in the story between and old sailor and the bookkeeper, were actually carried on by Kierkegaard himself. To an impartial observer this does not seem sufficient to prove Heiberg's right to maintain that Kierkegaard, in writing the bookkeeper's story, had personal experiences in view. Even in the case of so introspective an author as Kierkegaard presumably, in spite of all exaggerations, was, the observation that, in the description of a fictitious character, he ascribed to the latter experiences he had had himself and anxieties he had suffered from himself, does not warrant the opposite conclusion that then probably all the experiences and thoughts ascribed to the fictitious character were transferred from the author's own life. "It can be said", says Hans Brix in connection with this matter, "about the use of transmitted material in literary historical works with partly biographical contents that in numerous cases the scientific method takes the standpoint which Lyschander and his like stand for in history. A systematic critical evaluation of the sources with rejection of the material worth rejecting is not used. That unfounded but good anecdotes are included by way of illustration is not objectionable if only their functional character is maintained. But it is wrong to rely on loose and unverifiable traditions. They should be tested according to the rules of historical criticism and be rejected if they cannot prove their legitimacy, and it cannot be documented that the witness is entirely familiar with the case, is able to state it, and is actuated by the will to do so. Far too many idle tales have been committed to writing as good material in descriptions.—And one cannot select details out of an author's poetic works for the description of him, even if he has his own life in view, unless the thing can be documented, any more than one can call a folk song a historical source. It is therefore a gross error in method on Heiberg's part that, from analogies with the author's person, he takes from the story "A Possibility" the tale of a human catastrophe, introducing it into Kierkegaard's life, letting it stand for his personal experience in May 1836 with consequences for the whole of his future life."—The deepest cause why Heiberg's method of criticising the sources in so many cases proved imperfect and insufficient, so that wishful thinking and not proofs and arguments came to decide the truth value of the conjectures put forward, is to be found in the unfortunate interaction between his point of view and his method. His point of view was narrowly psychologico-historical which, scientifically, is unchallengable, but the narrowness was transferred to his method. In his treatment of the individual texts and their individual parts he failed to take into consideration their literary function, but tried to establish a direct connection between the fictional statements and the author's person, which is scientifically indefensible. Such a procedure will favour erroneous inferences and subjective decisions. The necessary condition for a successful result of the examination of a poetical work from the point of view of the author's psychology is that a sympathetic understanding of the idea and composition of the work is introduced as an intermediate link between the author and his production. This can be done with advantage even if it is known with certainty that the work is autobiographical; if this certainty is not present it is absolutely necessary. For in that case an æsthetic interpretation will decide, not what material is historical, but what in all probability is not. The more it can be shown that the individual parts of a work are assimilated in the whole, that the form and content of the isolated account are determined by the context, that the detail serves a literary purpose, the less probability is there that the part, the account, the detail, reproduces a historical fact.

In the case under consideration Heiberg should then have started his psychological interpretation of the story "A Possibility" with a general explanation of the relation of the inserted parts to their fictive author, the Quidam of the tale of suffering, and a special investigation of the relation between the action and the psychological point of the bookkeeper's history. After such a literary analysis he would have been able to judge whether a personal historical interpretation of the story could be undertaken with profit.—Of the inserted parts of the tale of suffering Frater

Taciturnus says in his explanatory epistle to the reader: "In order to shed light on his (Quidam's) reserve I have allowed some sketches to enter into the diary in which he, as it were, gropes for an expression for his own reserve. Directly he never speaks, he cannot do that, but indirectly. Therefore they must also be understood indirectly." (6, 451). From this statement it appears that the six inserted pieces must be understood in relation to Quidam's reserve, must be regarded as his first attempt to understand the law governing his own melancholy; and because he does not understand himself, he does not describe a reticent person, he gropes after himself by setting up a series of possible forms of reserve, but it only makes an apparently essential difference that one is a ruler, the other a bookkeeper, and that their experiences and external circumstances differ greatly, for in one thing they resemble each other, in that the circumstances of their lives have been a cause of their melancholy reticence. "With all the heroes I see in imagination it is more or less the case that deeply hidden they bear a sorrow into which they cannot or will not initiate anybody" (6, 209). The result of the outlined investigation will then be that an interpretation of the six inserted pieces must start from the concept "reticence" and attempt to survey the various forms in which this psychological phenomenon manifests itself. Such an investigation will inform us of the stages of Quidam's meditations on himself in that crisis of intensification which according to his own statement is in progress during the whole history of the betrothal. In his Kierkegaard studies Emanuel Hirsch has tried to set up such a scheme of classification (I. pp. 188-89); what is of interest here, however, is not so much the scheme itself as the opportuneness of the attempt. It may become a means of calculating the probable relation of the inserted pieces to Kierkegaard's own history. For when it turns out that the six tales serve the one purpose of shedding light on reticence in its various manifestations, then it may be inferred that the account of the histories of the melancholy heroes is conditioned by their special sufferings; it has formed the starting point for a construction of their lives, which must therefore as a whole be considered to be remote from reality. This general conjecture as to the genesis of the inserted pieces is confirmed by an examination of the bookkeeper's history. Among Søren Kierkegaard's papers there is a draft for the story which runs as follows: "Disposition. A man has once in his early youth in an excited state let himself be prevailed upon to visit a prostitute. It has all been forgotten. Now he wishes to marry. Then fear awakes. The possibility that he might be a father, that somewhere in the world there might live a being that owed its life to him, torments him day and night. He can confide in no one, he does not possess reliable knowledge of the fact himself.—It must therefore have happened at a prostitute's in the wild aimlessness of youth; if he had been a little in love, or it had been an actual seduction, he could not be conceived to be so ignorant, but now it is this very ignorance which constitutes the uneasiness of his anguish. On the other hand, just because of the recklessness of the whole affair, real impetus will only be given to his doubt when he actually falls in love" (IV, A 65). From this draft it appears with all clarity that it is the bookkeeper's unhappy state of mind when his soul is harassed by irrefutable suspicions which is the nucleus of the story. The dreary erotic affair is deduced from his psychological situation, and not the reverse. The debauchery must have taken place at a prostitute's, in the opposite case he could obtain certainty as to the justness of his suspicion and rid himself of his anxiety. In the final shape of the story the bookkeeper's utter inability to ascertain the consequences of his dissipations is further explained by the fact that he was drunk on the evening of the action, and that his friends had gone to America. It is Hans Brix who with his usual ingenuity has made clear the genesis of "A Possibility" and thus definitely exploded Heiberg's theory. His account of the case terminates in the following conclusion: "It is hereby fully documented that the history of the symposium and the momentary association with an unknown and untraceable bought woman has been developed by Kierkegaard as a simple consequence of what was the aim of the story: the account of a man who cannot know with certainty whether he may not perhaps be the father of a child. But since the account is thus seen to be constructed and composed from a purely invented literary topic it is a matter of course that it did not spring from nor is an account of an element in Kierkegaard's life" (Analyses and Problems III, p. 293). This conception of Brix's thus fully agrees with the above explanation of the inserted pieces. And so it turns out that both an immanent and a transcendental investigation of them leads to the same result that they are not directly connected with Søren Kierkegaard's intimate history.

In the above survey of Heiberg's production it has not been mentioned that the honour of, or the responsibility for, the discovery of those events and crises which in the "Episode" and the "Segment" he introduces into Kierkegaard's youthful years, does not fall undivided to his share. Nor does this appear from Heiberg's books; there are no references in them to works of other Kierkegaard researchers, no foot-notes where he acknowledges his indebtedness to his colleagues. This must have been a principle with Heiberg, for the results he submits in the "Episode" and the "Segment" are not the fruit of his investigations alone.

A. B. DRACHMANN, in his article (Tilskueren 1910; Udv. Afh. p. 175 ff.) which appeared when the first volume of the Papers was published, already called attention to the fact that the year 1835 shows a remarkable change in Søren Kierkegaard's interests; in the course of 1835 he turned from divinity and devoted himself to extensive æsthetic studies, primarily of the Faustus legend and its various adaptations. This observation from which Drachmann, however, does not draw any conclusion, is supported by VALDEMAR AMMUNDSEN (1875-1936, Professor of Theology in the University of Copenhagen) in the sober treatise "Søren Kierkegaards Ungdom. Hans Slægt og hans religiøse Udvikling" (Søren Kierkegaard's Youth. His Family and his Religious Development. Commemorative Publication of the University 1912). It is especially the three last chapters which are of interest in this connection. In the first three all the statements and informations about Kierkegaard as a child and schoolboy, about his family, especially his father, which it has been possible to glean from Kierkegaard's own papers, from memoirs and public and private records, are submitted. In this way not a little that is new has been brought to light, but beyond the fact, which has played a certain part in the discussion about the "earthquake", that the old hosier, five months after his second wedding and eighteen months after his first wife's death, was made happy by the birth of a son, the chapters contain nothing sensational; what they bring of documents of essential importance for the understanding of Kierkegaard's development, had all been published previously, though indeed not in one collection, and the greater part of them by far not in as irreproachable a way as here. Ammundsen's reproduction of letters and documents is throughout correct, whereas his commentaries are brief and on the whole cautious; they do not break with the tradition, but rather serve as guiding transitional links between the lengthy quotations. To collect and edit in a faultless manner, to supply a document concerning Kierkegaard's family history and childhood, was the task Ammundsen wished to solve in the first section of his treatise.—The last three chapters deal with Kierkegaard's development in his undergraduate days. After an introductory explanation of the state of affairs in the theological faculty at the time when Kierkegaard began to attend lectures at the University, an able account is given of the criticism of the prevailing forms of teaching Christianity which Søren Kierkegaard entered in his notebooks at the close of 1834 and the beginning of 1835. He could not reconcile himself either to Grundtvigianism, rationalism, or orthodoxy, and in the spring of 1835 he seems to have done with Christianity in the forms in which it presented itself to him. Ammundsen then passes on to an investigation of Kierkegaard's development in the period from the summer of 1835 to the spring of 1838, that is to say, the period which Heiberg has treated in the "Segment". The two chapters are entitled „Attempt at Consolidation in the Summer of 1835" and "Gliding—Fall—Awakening", and describe the transition from the cheerful resolve at Gilleleje via the stop, the shock, the period of dissipation (Ammundsen had borrowed the "Episode" in manuscript, cf. his book p. 121) to the incipient rise in the latter part of the autumn 1837, culminating in the religious awakening on May 19, 1838.—In its main features it is the same course of development which is described in Heiberg's "Segment", but Ammundsen has no ambition in the way of microscopy or continuity. His account is purely annalistic, registering, does not look for causes. The chief data are given and the notes which unambiguously testify to Kierkegaard's contact with Christianity. The tradition which had already then grown up with respect to the "earthquake" and the interpretation of the inserted pieces in the "Stages" are adopted in principle without reserve, and the episode constructed by Heiberg is inserted. Of value, though far from exhausting the material, are those parts of Ammundsen's book which deal with Kierkegaard's university time, the period to 1836, which none of his predecessors had tried to map out. And it is here that Ammundsen has extended Drachmann's above-mentioned observation to a demonstration of a crisis in Kierkegaard's relation to Christianity. In the course of the autumn of 1835 there comes a pause in the rising movement, and immediately after it comes the offence. "While Søren Kierkegaard's objections were previously mostly directed against one or the other conception of Christianity they are now aimed at Christianity itself at a rapidly increasing rate" (p. 115). With a note on November 3 about the tolerance of Christianity of fresh air, remarks on religious subjects disappear for over six months.

It is this trustworthy account of the sudden changes of current in the mind of the young Søren Kierkegaard which Hans Ellekilde (b. 1891, folklorist) four years later tries to elaborate in his paper on the "Earthquake" (Danske Studier 1916, pp. 1-44). Ellekilde applies the same principles of research as Heiberg in the "Episode"; he assumes that it is in life as in the novels where there is always an external cause in the form of happy or unhappy events that makes the hero change his mind concerning the ordering of existence: the drastic changes in Søren Kierkegaard's view of life must have been produced by an event, a personal tragedy. And he brings to light what this tragedy is by comparing Kierkegaard's notes in his diaries with his production, especially the note about the "Earthquake" and "Solomon's Dream", which, as we know, already Brandes connected. Concerning this combination of the presumably autobiographical and the obviously fictional text we refer the reader to our criticism of Heiberg's method above; here we shall merely briefly review the results Ellekilde thinks he has arrived at by his investigations. "In the autumn of 1835, perhaps in the night between the 10th and 11th of October, Søren Kierkegaard accidentally saw that his father in the contrition of his heart prostrated himself before God and penitently poured out his sins: his childhood's cursing of God, and his manhood's sexual offence. And to the son, who nourished the profoundest respect and admiration for his father, this must have been a discovery which turned his love to a shocked indignation with his father and also led him to a shocked indignation with God. For the insight which the earthquake gave him into his father's life forced on him a new, infallible rule of interpretation of all the phenomena, his father's wealth, and the frequent deaths in the family. The temporal happiness must be regarded as a curse. The whole family was subject to God's punishment, and was to be wiped out by God's mighty hand like an unsuccessful experiment, and the old hosier himself go to his grave as the last of his line. And Søren Kierkegaard felt the silence of death grow around him and was indignant with God who punishes the innocent instead of the guilty. And the appalling realisation of this threw him in to the arms of dread and drove him to that life of dissipation which in 1836 ended in the visit to the brothel about which he later wrote: "—perhaps my aberrations were not so atrocious in God's eyes, for it was dread that made me err." What, more precisely, should be understood by this can be gathered from a serious study of his work "The Concept of Dread", a book which, in spite of its ponderous philosophical equipment, is by no means, as supposed by the philosophers, a philosophical work in an objective scientific sense— — —, no, it is on the contrary in the deepest sense a subjective work, a personal book in the most intimate sense, which primarily, first and last, must be understood psychologically, humanly." (p. 29).—It appears with all clarity from the above reports, not least from the lines last quoted, that a co-operation has taken place between Heiberg and contemporary enquirers, even so close that Heiberg was literally able to obtain directives for his continued work in Ellekilde's studies on Søren Kierkegaard's youth.

B. "Social" Psychology

Shortly before Christmas 1929 FRITHIOF BRANDT (b. 1892), Professor of Philosophy in the University of Copenhagen, issued the voluminous work "The Young Søren Kierkegaard"; it was the second large work of a now rather extensive production which, besides a thesis for the doctorate on Thomas Hobbes and some textbooks on philosophy, includes a number of works on purely literary and artistic subjects. At its appearance the book caused not a little sensation, differing as it did from its forerunners of the kind by being diffuse and detailed in documentation, easily readable, thrilling and amusing, and polemics and criticism followed in its wake. When surprise at the general impression had subsided, one began to turn over the details, and little by little it became clear that essential combinations and arguments were not proof against criticism. But apart from a wide distrust of the individual results of the investigation, its fundamental view of Søren Kierkegaard as a man who in an almost normal way needed contact with and was inspired by his milieu has ousted his predecessors' conception of him as "a solitary fir, egotistically self-contained, and aiming high." In the series of critical and supplementary articles and papers provoked by Brandt's book his fundamental thesis has been maintained, and his work of finding new sources and combining them with the "Papers" has been continued by others, and this has led to the clearing up of a number of the obscure points in Kierkegaard's biography. Thus the fruitfulness of the new point of view has been proved.

The germ of Brandt's voluminous book is a note in the diary which Kierkegaard entered on July 21, 1839, immediately after the publication of Henrik Hertz's novel "Stemninger og Tilstande" (Moods and Situations): "Now I can understand why H. Hertz was so anxious to talk to me, now that I read his last handiwork with political fancies and sallies. It is a pity though that he has left out the Interpreter's satirical fancies which, to be sure, he believes could be done without damage to the main contents, but I think that it was the best part and ought hardly, I suppose, to be left out merely from a dramatic interest in the Interpreter's character, but there has probably been very good reasons for it; for Hertz is not equal to that" (II, A 508). This note gave Brandt the clue to the fact that Hertz had used Søren Kierkegaard as his model for one of the characters occurring in his book, called the Interpreter. And this discovery brought others, no less sensational, in its train. It turned out that the Copenhagen writers in the time from 1836 to 1843 spent a great deal of their time and talents on portraying each other, and that no less than three had tried their hand at Søren Kierkegaard. The documentation of these assertions fills the main part of Brandt's treatise; here we shall merely indicate the line it takes and state its chief results.

In "Moods and Situations" the author describes a set consisting of five bachelors who dine together at Mrs. Børresen's dining-rooms in Vestergade. One of these is the Interpreter. The description of his appearance and behaviour and his political views agrees so exactly with the picture we can form from the tradition of the young Søren Kierkegaard's mental and physical apparition that it can be established that the Interpreter is an actual portrait of Søren Kierkegaard. A closer inspection shows that the other diners too are drawn from historical persons, Assessor P. V. Jacobsen, Hans Andersen, P. L. Møller, and finally Hertz himself, having served as models for the figures Harriet, Amadis, Verner, and Thomsen. An investigation of the data of the historical persons further shows that Hertz in his description of the individual figures keeps quite close to the facts, and there is reason to believe, therefore, that the part of the novel dealing with the dining-place in Vestergade is simply realistic history-writing. If this presumption is correct we have in "Moods and Situations" an important source of information about Kierkegaard's way of life and his circle of acquaintances in the critical years of his youth. Starting from the relation of the Interpreter to the individual members of the set Brandt therefore tries to clear up Kierkegaard's actual relation to the four men and to unravel the psychological and literary significance of his acquaintance with them.—The relation between Harriet and the Interpreter (i.e. between P. V. Jacobsen and Kierkegaard) is described by Hertz so as to be almost identical with the relation between Assessor Wilhelm and his young friend the æsthetic A. The former, who stands for dignified gravity, sober judgment and clarified humanism, by his mere presence acts as a damper on the Interpreter's nature which otherwise principally manifests itself in sarcasm and mordant irony. This observation warrants the presumption that P. V. Jacobsen was the model for the author of Either-Or's ethical part. Harriet is the only one of the set whom the Interpreter shows respect. For the others at the table he has on the whole only scorn left and is especially merciless towards the imaginative and naive Amadis. If we may venture to regard Hertz's descriptions as historically reliable we here have a piece of information about the relation between Kierkegaard and Hans Andersen which may serve as an explanation of certain peculiarities in the later production of the two famous men. Previous Kierkegaard researchers have advanced various conjectures as to what might be the reason why Søren Kierkegaard in "Of the Papers of a person still among the living" attacked Andersen so severely both as an author and as a man, especially since he had promised him a sympathetic judgment, and critics have been puzzled about the parrot in "The Goloshes of Fortune" since it could be seen that it was a Heibergian, but not which one. Brandt now advances the double conjecture that in the sarcastic and witty parrot Andersen drew a picture of Søren Kierkegaard in return for his personal, insulting remarks, and that Søren Kierkegaard, in his anger at the parrot, sharpened his criticism of Andersen's production and followed it up with attacks on his person. —A somewhat similar personal quarrel between Kierkegaard and P. L. Møller, according to Brandt, seems to be the explanation of the violence of their clash in 1845. For the clearing up of these circumstances Hertz has only an insignificant contribution since the only inference that can be drawn from his novel is that Kierkegaard and P. L. Møller were personally acquainted. But a close examination of Goldschmidt's characterisation of Møller in "Recollections" and in the novel "Homeless", of Møller's literary remains, and of the information that has come down to us of his reputation in the Copenhagen of those days, renders it probable that Søren Kierkegaard modelled his Seducer on Møller's figure. And a closer inspection of the later remarks of the two writers confirms the conjecture. Møller's sarcastic review of "Guilty—Not Guilty", in which Kierkegaard describes his own engagement, must be interpreted as a reply to the indiscretion of which Kierkegaard had been guilty in using Møller's person and erotic principles as his model when he wrote the "Seducer's Diary". "Just as Kierkegaard in his preface to the "Seducer's Diary" speaks his mind about his fellow æsthete P. L. Møller, thus also in "Gæa" P. L. Møllers speaks his mind about Kierkegaard on the basis of his love story. The parallelism in their judgment of each other is striking. They both think of each other that they are ill, and that their behaviour approximates to the criminal" (p. 276). The ultimate and last evidence of the identity of Møller and Johannes which Brandt gives is the fact that Kierkegaard's judgment of Johannes' moral person in "Unscientific Postcript" is mercilessly severe, while in "Either—Or" he seems to be somewhat puzzled as to whether or not Johannes is wicked. This change or increased severity of Søren Kierkegaard's judgment can only be explained by the fact that Møller, in the period from 1845 to 1846, had developed in such a way that there could no longer be any doubt about his moral depravity. In "Unscientific Postscript" Kierkegaard writes: "Johannes the Seducer is damnation in coldness, a "marked" and extinct individuality". This merciless judgment can hardly be passed on the basis of the Seducer's Diary. Brandt thinks that Søren Kierkegaard deliberately formed his sentence so that the literary contemporaries could be in no doubt as to whom it was aimed at. For in the years between "Either—Or" and "Unscientific Postcript" Møller "finally fell to a level that definitely and hopelessly unclassed him, and Kierkegaard evidently knew of this" (p. 278).

This exhausts Hertz's description of the Interpreter's relation to the various guests at Mrs. Børresen's private table, but one more element in the book seems to be of interest for the research on Kierkegaard. At the instance of Amadis and Verner the circle one evening decide to have a banquet. It begins very festively but in the case of four of the participants concludes with heavy intoxication. Before it begins the Interpreter has stolen away. Brandt submits an extensive material consisting of restaurant receipts and topographical details to prove that it was the same bachelors' feast Søren Kierkegaard had in mind when he wrote "In vino veritas", and he proved by comparing the two symposia that in the main they merely differ by their intellectual content while they have the externalities in common—with the exception of the giver of the feast. This, according to Brandt, was Kierkegaard, and the restaurant receipt for 235 rixdollars which constituted a large item in the heavy bill presented to the old hosier in the autumn of 1837 is supposed to date from the sumptuous symposium taking place in the summer of 1836.

The last section of Brandt's book deals with Kierkegaard's relation to Poul Martin Møller, and in excitement it outdoes all literary historical treatises and the greater part of the works of fiction written in this country. The starting point is Kierkegaard's first redaction of the dedication of "The Concept of Dread", which book, as we know, is dedicated to Poul Møller. He is described in the dedication amongst other things as "the enthusiasm of my youth, the mighty trumpet of my awakening, the desired object of my mood, the confidant of my beginning, my lost friend, my missing reader." In this passage Brandt dwells especially on the words "the mighty trumpet of my awakening" and pronounces as his temporary conjecture that it was Møller's well-known remark, "You are so thoroughly polemical that it is quite appalling," which caused Kierkegaard's awakening, and that it took place on the 4th June 1836. This hypothesis is verified in a round-about way.—In 1835—37 Poul Møller made some notes for a literary work which was never written. The drafts consist of 15 notes entitled "The Ahasuerus Fragments". The figure that appears to us from these notes is "a philosopher thoroughly polemical, polemical both in regard to contemporary philosophy and ordinary life and its people. He does not want to do anything though he realises how considerable his talents are. He is a penetrating observer, inclined to discussion, and may be dramatic in his behaviour. Nothing is spontaneous about him. World-weariness lies behind it all" (p. 364). Brandt supposes that Møller drew his Ashasuerus with the young Kierkegaard for his model and finds confirmation of this by an examination of Kierkegaard's own notes from the period 1835-37, which not only frequently deal with Ashasuerus but in the main ascribe the same psychic qualities to him as characterise Poul Møller's figure.—Kierkegaard's Ashasuerus notes lead Brandt on to an independent investigation of the connection between Kierkegaard's romantic studies in his youth and his later production. From Heiberg's "Segment" it will be remembered that in his undergraduate days Kierkegaard occupied himself with the three legendary medieval figures: Don Juan, Faustus, and the Wandering Jew, and that he felt a kinship in mind and fate with the last-mentioned. Brandt carries on Heiberg's investigation and—before he reverts to the relation between Poul Møller and Kierkegaard—tries to explain the significance of Kierkegaard's studies and his feeling of personal relationship to the three legendary figures for the architecture of the æsthetic stage. Don Juan, Faustus, and Ahasuerus are like snapshot figures, without relation to the ethical or religious, the main types of the æsthetic stage, representing respectively enjoyment, doubt, and despair. "Only Don Juan did Kierkegaard contrive to execute fully, the modern Don Juan with P. L. Møller as his model. But behind Kierkegaard's poetical description of himself as the æsthete A lies Ahasuerus. This gave the basic view of Kierkegaard's own understanding of his "æsthetic" period which lasted till the breaking off of his engagement in his twenty-eighth year: that he was Ahasuerus, a despairing man, and that at bottom his despair was to be understood as religious, as in the case of the real Ahasuerus" (p. 448).—That Søren Kierkegaard was an Ahasuerus was seen by Poul Møller, this is evidenced by his Ahasuerus fragments which give a deep insight into the young Kierkegaard's soul even if they do not penetrate to the last darkness. And Poul Møller let Kierkegaard know his opinion of him, Brandt maintains; under what circumstances and with what consequences he thinks himself able to show by means of a collation of Møller's fragments, Hertz's notes, Kierkegaard's diary notes and the draft for an undergraduate drama "The Battle between the Old Soap-cellar and the New Soap-cellar" which is found among his papers. Brandt's hypothesis is, briefly, to this effect: On June the 4th 1836 Kierkegaard met Hertz and Poul Møller at a party at J. L. Heiberg's. Hertz delighted the guests with witty remarks which, however, he had not invented himself but borrowed from Kierkegaard. The latter was annoyed and tried to revenge himself by outdoing Hertz in wit and dialectical mockery, by polemising against him, i.e. actually against himself. At this juncture Poul Møller broke into the conversation, bursting out to Kierkegaard: "You are so thoroughly polemical that it is quite appalling". "These words hit Kierkegaard hard an made a deep impression on him. He was at the end of a long critical period where the joking devil had played his pranks." He went home, meditating suicide. "Fortunately the suicide did not materialise. Instead, the outburst caused that awakening which he recollects in his dedication to Poul Møller, and the character of which can be followed step by step in the diary from the 6th June" (p. 438).

Brandt's book has met with much criticism; almost every step in the process of his work from the introductory reading of the manuscripts to the concluding constructions, has been tested. The majority of expert objections are concerned with details of analyses and combinations; the critical work therefore has not led to any collective rectifying result but to a large number of small corrections. In itself it was not remarkable if the critics of "The Young Søren Kierkegaard" possessed more detailed knowledge of a number of the subjects discussed than the author, for a multiplicity of the most heterogeneous passages from the literature of the 1830s and 40s are embodied in the material; but the corrective remarks are remarkable by their great number and their uniformity. Common to them all is that they prove or render probable that the texts which Brandt has by some pressure brought within the narrow bounds of Søren Kierkegaard's private history may without constraint be understood in a larger cultural and literary historical connection. Where Brandt uses remarks, notes, and poetical works to place Kierkegaard in a human environment, his critics try to understand the same parts of the text separately, in their literary setting. Behind this difference in the trend of the interpretation there is no different intention but a difference in the view of literature.

In the epilogue to his book Brandt outlines his theory of literature especially with a view to the relation between a literary work and its source of inspiration: "In the most recent research on literature a school has grown up which with much greater energy than before points to the significance of earlier literature for the genesis of later literature. Often this school has the effect of a reaction against the school that looks for life and experience as a basis for the literary work. If previously it was said that literature arises out of life, it is now said that literature arises out of literature.—Both points of view are of course justifiable as elements of understanding but must be regarded precisely as elements. They only explain the genesis of a literary work to a certain extent, and the less the more original the writer is. Inferior art is most easily "explained", e.g. the art which is only a tracing of reality ("Moods and Situations" is a good example), and that which is only literary literature, an impersonal imitation. In great art the factor is added which we call the author's personality, and this is precisely the irrational factor which none of the above-mentioned viewpoints can reach, what Kierkegaard himself called "the birthmark of personality" which exhibits itself both in the form and the contents of a work of art. But how much the personal factor has asserted itself can really only be decided when the two points of view have been adopted and it has been seen how much can be explained. Personality is the costly residue that remains when the rest has been filtered off" (p. 450).

The contrast between literature and life as angles of interpretation which is here laid down seems in some degree to be due to an underrating of the literary view applied in modern æsthetics. The borrowing of subjects is not, any more than the writer's personal experience, of primary interest to it. The work is the central thing. And it must be understood in its entirety before the intention of its parts can be explained. But the understanding of any historical work requires a knowledge of the tradition within which it came into existence, from tradition in a narrower sense, the immediate culture-historical situation of the genres, ideas, and types, according to which the authors have formed themselves, in imitation or opposition, to tradition in a wider sense, the sum of impersonal knowledge of the most different things that the writer has acquired in his capacity of citizen, reader of newspapers, and theatre-goer in a definite historical setting.

Such an æsthetic-historical analysis, the purpose of which is the understanding of the text in its contemporaneity must precede any attempt at explanation, for only in this way will the enquirer obtain a valid material, in this way the meaning of words and turns of speech is apprehended, the function and interrelation of the parts within the whole:

or conversely the problems are uncovered, the lack of coherence, unequal distribution of energy etc. In both instances the results gained can then be traced back to the author's personality, and it can be ascertained what impressions he has tried, successfully or unsuccessfully, to fuse in the artistic expression; in the artistic expression in which the author's personality must be supposed to be present undivided in borrowed and experienced and invented material; as Søren Kierkegaard says himself: "I am indeed of opinion that theft in the world of the spirit is not only unallowable but actually impossible———" (VIII, 2; B 7 p. 30).

With support in the available criticism I shall now go through a number of the decisive arguments in two of the chapters of the book.—In the chapter on P. L. Møller it is argued that Søren Kierkegaard used him as a model when he wrote "The Seducer's Diary". A temporary analysis of the first part of "Either—Or" forms the introduction; starting from A's mystifying foreword to the diary, a cleavage of the æsthete into two persons is made, A and Johannes, each representing a creation within the æsthetic stage. What is gained by this is not quite clear for no one has ever thought that A and Johannes were identical, but that Johannes' diary was composed by A as one of the "numerous attempts at an æsthetic view of life", which his papers are said to contain. And this view neither excludes the possibility that Johannes one-sidedly represents pleasure and thus a particular creation, nor that he is drawn from a living model. But the conjecture that the unifying principle in the first volume of "Either—Or" should be the æsthetic stage and not the æsthete, a philosophical category and not a person, conflicts with the fundamental idea of the book. While writing it Søren Kierkegaard made a note (III, B 177) of the plan of the book and its connection with the principle of contradiction in which he says: "It would not therefore be æsthetically right to write in this work a treatise on the prinicple of contradiction; no, it is maintained personally —". A and B must be regarded as the two persons whose existences as contradictory contrasts exclude one another. That they are persons, "existing individualities", and not stages to be chosen between, is precisely "the indirect polemic of the book against speculation" (7, 238). Hence it must be maintained that Johannes comes under A; the relation between them could at the outset be supposed to be as between Quidam and the insertions. In this way too Johannes Climacus interprets it: "Even the Seducer's Diary was merely the possibility of terror conjured up by the æsthete in his groping existence just because without actually being anything he had to try everything as a possibility" (7, 283 footnote).

Apart from the plan of "Either—Or" the prerequisite for the model-hypothesis is, however, that Søren Kierkegaard and Møller knew each other. That at the time of the clash in 1845 they had a fairly good surface acquaintance with each other is certain enough; both of them were then prominent authors with a motley reputation in the small Copenhagen. The proof that they had previously (before the writing of the "Seducer's Diary" in 1842), and more intimately, known each other is "Moods and Situations", in which, as we saw, Verner was supposed to be identical with P. L. Møller. That he was, is Brandt's "subjective conviction"; but Sejer Kühle (cf. p. 111) has shown, by an examination of Hertz's study notes for the novel, that it was his plan to "introduce a young person who is dissolute and witty like Jørgen Jørgensen", a pretty well known and harmless Bohemian of the Copenhagen of the time. The final forming of Verner deviates somewhat from this plan, and altogether the figure is without firm outlines; but if drawn from a live model, that model must be supposed to have been Jørgensen. And Hertz seems not to have become acquainted with Møller till the 1840s, when he received letters from him addressed with great perfection of form to "Most honoured Mr. Hertz" and signed "Yours most respectfully, P. L. Møller." Similar negative evidence of an old acquaintance between Møller and Kierkegaard is further found among the latter's papers. During his meditations on the Corsair feud he wrote in 1849: "Take Goldschmidt, or P. L. Møller, would any of them personally have ventured to insult me or merely to be uncivil; no, in a personal situation they would show politeness, even distinguished (politeness)" (X, 1; A 475). Finally Brandt's "perhaps most conclusive proof that Verner is Møller", namely that in 1843 Møller in a defensive pamphlet stated that "in his literary state of innocence he was by no means distinguished for what in Østergade and Vestergade is called "a morally correct behaviour""; Brandt regards the words as an allusion to Mrs. Børresen's premises which in the novel are situated in Vestergade but "in fact" were to be found in Østergade, and to the judgment passed on him by the set. A couple of quotation marks have at some earlier period fallen out. Professor Hans Brix has pointed out in his criticism that "Østergade and Vestergade" was a comedy by Th. Overskou published in 1828 which amongst others contained the expression "a morally correct behaviour".

Assuming that all hypotheses had been sufficiently proved so far, the main thing would nevertheless be to prove that Møller was the model for the Seducer. In Søren Kierkegaard's terminology Johannes was a conscious seducer, a modern type corresponding to the medieval direct seducer, Don Juan. Møller seems to have been of that type. Brandt adduces a long series of more or less doubtful correspondences between Møller's production and "The Seducer's Diary"; he does not think that anything can be inferred from this, but that the pieces compared have a strong affinity. The point to be proved is that Søren Kierkegaard's description of the reflective seducer, the æsthetic type, trends towards that particular characteristic individual P. L. Møller. It is such conclusive evidence that Brandt thinks he can find in the contrast between the epigrammatically short and clear condemnation of Johannes in "Unscientific Postcript" and the vague appraisal of his moral character in the foreword to the "Seducer's Diary". The change, he thinks, can only be explained on the assumption that Søren Kierkegaard, when he formulated his pithy judgment of Johannes, had P. L. Møller in mind. For Johannes, as we know, had not changed in the years 1843—46, but Møller had changed; he had in this period fallen into a degradation that definitely and irremediably unclassed him. This explanation of the increased severity of judgment is due to a simplification in the presentation of the problem. A difference in two judgments of the same person must either be due to a change in the person judged, or in the judge. But in the fictive world in which Johannes is judged he is precisely the constant, while the judgment is referred to two different persons: in 1843 Johannes is judged by a fellow æsthete, to whom it may be said: "Once you said with your usual foolhardiness that one could not blame Nero for setting fire to Rome to gain some idea of the burning of Troy, but we must ask whether he really had art enough to understand how to enjoy it. Now it is one of your imperial fancies never to avoid any thought, never to be frightened by it" (2, 200); in 1846 the Seducer is judged by the pseudonym of the highest stage but one in the system of stages. That the former should be vague on ethical questions is not only reasonable but just as necessary as a representative of religiousness A having a moral conviction and the will to live up to it.

However, on the assumption that the latter explanation is the correct one, Johannes Climacus's distinctive judgment: "Johannes the Seducer is damnation in coldness, a "marked" and extinct individuality", must also be capable of being understood directly, without any use of private knowledge. On a closer inspection of Brandt's interpretation of it, it proves doubtful as regards the understanding of the characterising words. Brandt says: "It seems likely that Kierkegaard, with his strange expression about Johannes that he was an extinct individuality, may be referring to this peculiarity (the loss of social prestige in 1843—46) of Møller's. The words, I suppose, must mean that Johannes is played out, that one cannot count on him any more. It also seems to me obvious that this judgment cannot be passed on Johannes as he is described by Kierkegaard in the "Seducer's Diary". Whatever we think of Johannes, extinct he is not, and he is also, in spite of vacillating objection, treated with no little formal respect (p. 279). And in connection with the discussion of an unknown "actual error" of an erotic kind, which in 1843 brought Møller into public disrepute, we read: "It is said in the final judgment of Johannes that he is a "marked" individuality; the word is made very prominent by quotation marks. However ambiguous the term is we are not left in doubt that here Kierkegaard—in a certain contrast to the Seducer's Diary—regards Johannes as definitely branded. This shows a suspiciously good agreement with Møller's degradation in these years. From Goldschmidt's account we understand that the "actual error" was generally known in the form of rumour at the time" (p. 281). Under the verb "mærke", "mark", the "Dictionary of the Danish Language", amongst other quotations has this: "One should beware of "marked" men, i.e. red-haired, squinting, hunch-backed persons", i.e. with the word "marked" in quotation marks, as in Kierkegaard, in the superstitious use of the word "marked" (by God's finger) with disfiguring external physical defects. If we assume that Søren Kierkegaard wrote in such a way that his use of the language was understandable without employing the small Copenhagen shortsight glasses, then such a disfigurement must be looked for in Johannes. And curiously enough, about Johannes' appearance we know nothing but that at the time when the seduction was almost accomplished it was to his indignation blemished by such a disfigurement. "It is curious enough, I notice at present with grief that I am getting the betraying sign which Horace wishes for every unfaithful girl—a black tooth, a front tooth into the bargain. How superstitious one can be" (1, 458). The other annotated word, extinct, Søren Kierkegaard uses in "The Concept of Dread" in a sense that in a far deeper way characterises a seducer than the possible failure of his bourgeois happiness. In the chapter on the demoniac "dread of the good" it is explained that the reticent person has broken off all communication with the world around him; in this way he has broken the continuity of his life, his relation to time and that which exists in time; and only the good can—in a Kierkegaardian sense—bear a relation to time, have a history. In the light of continuity reticence is the sudden thing; but in his isolation the reticent person can establish an inner pseudo-continuity. "The continuity corresponding to the sudden thing is what might be called extinction. For tediousness, extinction, are a continuity in nothing" (4, 442). Taken in this sense the word extinct brings the seducer with all his erotic diaries, "Commentarius perpetuus", under a psychological formula.

In the chapter on Hans Andersen it is likewise the hardness and especially the supposed increased severity of the Kierkegaardian judgment which Brandt tries to explain. He gives his conjecture the following form: "Just as Søren Kierkegaard was working at his criticism of Andersen "The Goloshes of Fortune" appeared (19/5 1838), with the satirical portrait. "When Kierkegaard began his treatise he was perhaps in a kinder frame of mind, but the parrot caused a change. Instead of giving a balanced æsthetic appreciation, Kierkegaard's book, imperfectly veiled under the mask of criticism, has in great part become a commentary on the parrot and a merciless exposure of Andersen's person, an act of revenge" (p. 126). One feels an urge to protest in the name of reason and decency; this is not the way it happens. Even humans can be underrated. And at any rate cogent proofs, preferably confessions, are required before we can hope to hit the mark on aiming so low. There exist no confessions. But it is with this section as with that on Møller, it is made up of many details which in themselves are problematic and may take us along many paths. Here we shall merely discuss Brandt's analysis and judgment of "From the Papers of a still Living Author". The book is reviewed twice on pp. 136-44, first on two pages the general aspect, and then on five pages in more detail "the main points of the book", i.e. the section on Andersen. The account is thus marked by Brandt's express resolve to regard the book from the angle that it *is* Søren Kierkegaard's reply to the parrot (136). Brandt dwells on the insults and disregards the coherence. But there is a coherence, though it is only loose. The composition is rigid and yet the main sections only seem formally connected with each other. The typographically unbroken text can be divided as follows: A. The now characteristic will to begin from the beginning everywhere, which in philosophy (with comparative justice) has manifested itself in Hegel and Hamann, in politics (as an objectionable assault on reality) in the arrogant, unjustly self-confident, and in the impatient who feel powerless in the face of the circumstances of life, and finally in fiction in the author of the "Tales of Everyday Life" who represents a standpoint of religious resignation won by reflection and experience, and in Blicher who represents a poetical atmosphere, a deep and spontaneous originality (13, 57—66). B.a. The total impression of Andersen as "a possibility of a personality entangled in a web of casual moods, who to become such (i.e. a personality) requires a vigorous vital development", as a poet who after his beginning as a lyrist has skipped his epic (i.e. failed to embrace seriously a given reality) (66-67). b. Andersen's relation to the above-mentioned trends of the time: the political which by its platitudinarious character has promoted his lyrical subjectivity, precipitating him into the funnel of his own personality; the philosophical, with which he has not been in touch at all; the literary, with which he has occupied himself less as a reader than as a future novelist (67-71). c. The genesis of Andersen's novels seems to have resulted from the fact that his poetic desires, ousted from the world, take refuge in his imagination, but his personal resentment at the real world is then transferred to his imaginary figures; in this way a double light falls on his novels. The cause is the absence of a view of life which is actually Providence in the novel, the deeper unity" (71-81). d. The consequence of this lack shown by examples from Andersen's novels in general (81-92). e. And by examples from "Only a Fiddler", especially from the principal character (92-99). Conclusion (99—100).—This exposition, which moves downwards by degrees from the description of the general outlook of the time to the most special in Andersen's novels would seem to be meant to show how defects of the time and defects in Andersen have combined to hamper his development. Andersen has too copious poetical gifts to become lost in politics; but faced with the two possibilities: objective resignation and subjective spontaneity, it is seen that he has not a sufficiently pronounced talent to be rescued by the latter, and the former he has neglected. He is thus still a possibility to whom the way across "the bridge of sighs" to an ethical religious development of personality is open. The germs of "Either—Or" are here divined.

What relation does this exposition bear to Søren Kierkegaard's person? We are told in the conclusion that he can reanimate in his mind the moods which he experienced as a reader of Andersen's novels, so "that the totality of them assemble as for a leavetaking in one concentration in a present which yet at the same moment feels in itself the necessity of becoming a past, and thus evokes in me a certain wistful smile as I regard them, a feeling of gratitude when I remember the man to whom I owe it all, . . ." (99). If we compare this remark with the following æsthetic pronouncement, "that the poet must in the first place achieve an efficient personality himself, and that it is only this personality, thus dead and transfigured, which should and can produce, not the many-faceted earthly palpable one" (13-79), and again compare these two pronouncements with the contention in the introduction that two souls are contained in the author's body, one that sometimes "in blessed moments" communicates with the eternal and derives its ideas therefrom, and a practical wordly one through which the former communicates by telegraph with the world" (VII-VIII), then there seems to be a connection here suggesting that Søren Kierkegaards himself was at some stage of the road, which he recommended Andersen to take, between the moods of possibility which must now belong to the past, and the achievement of the dead and transfigured personality; hence that he himself was "a still living author". In support of this hypothesis it may be stated that Søren Kierkegaard, when 11 years later he prepared the publication of a paper on a related subject, "The Crisis, and a Crisis in the Life of an Actress" thought of giving it the subtitle "From the Papers of a Deceased Author" (VIII, 2; B 90,1). Then he had come to the end of the road.

This conjecture, incidentally, will agree with what Emanuel Hirsch pointed out, that in the summer of 1838 Søren Kierkegaard underwent a sudden religious development. Hirsch considers this observation sufficient to motivate the rejection of Brandt's explanation of Søren Kierkegaard's severer judgment, and he himself, after a detailed survey of the first book, advances the following conjecture: "Kierkegaard's judgment of Andersen's novel fell out as it did because Kierkegaard had undergone an inner experience between April and September 1838. When at the beginning of April he thought of introducing himself with an æsthetic criticism as a disciple of the late Poul Martin Møller, he may actually have chosen Andersen's "Fiddler" because, in spite of all emphatic contradiction, yet in the mood and attitude of the novel he felt something related to his own inner state of despair. When now with his appeal to Christendom he came in principle under the sway of a new, quite different, view of life, the kindly delimiting explanation must turn into a passionate repulsion. This has been a simply unavoidable event in which his private will has absolutely no share" (Kierkegaard Studien I, pp. 53-54).

The problems round Kierkegaard's criticism cannot, however, be said to have been solved with this. The disproportion between the strongly religious almost confessional portions and the merciless ragging of Andersen, the insufficient coherence altogether, is not explained. There is something disproportionate, unreleased, in the whole undertaking. This was felt too by contemporary readers. Hertz wrote in his diary after a conversation with Heiberg about the book: "Kierkegaard's book as regards Andersen (1838). It is a queer churchyard[1]. Judging by some few traces it would seem that the trumpet has been blown for resurrection from the graves.—But if so, the dead have not yet found their bones but are fighting about them. For the confusion is great. (The Mesopotamian language is a queer language)". (Personalhist. Tidsskrift 1932, p. 261). This utterance, only half interpretable, and evidently containing allusions to unknown conversations and perhaps to an incipient Christian awakening in Søren Kierkegaard observed by others, confirms the impression that a complicated uncompleted psychological process took place in Kierkegaard while he was writing the book.—The pointing out of these obscure relationships gives no positive result, but calling attention to them perhaps shows better than a verification that the piece with which Brandt thinks that he can complete the broken mosaic is too common and too lustreless.

Through the quotation from Hertz just mentioned, critics were able to penetrate into the part dealing with P. M. Møller. It is presumably the same Biblical trumpets which re-echo in Hertz's recording and in the epitaph with which Kierkegaard dedicates "The Concept of Dread" to the late P. M. Møller. But the discussion of details has already taken us too far afield. The above criticism of the two chapters on Hans Andersen and P. L. Møller must suffice to justify the verdict on Brandt's method and so a judgment of the book as a whole. Brandt's attempt to deepen the understanding of Kierkegaard's production by shedding light on the milieu in which he lived in his undergraduate days, and by calling attention to the controversies he may have had with a couple of his acquaintances, has failed in the main, because the material brought to light has been misused. Vilh. Andersen came to the same result after a critical perusal of Brandt's book. He writes in his review that Brandt "has meant to build a foundation wall under Søren Kierkegaards' castle in the air, and carried the foundation right up to the eaves", that Søren Kierkegaard's pseudonymous production is an airy castle but Brandt would turn it into a wax works, and he declares that the source of these encroachments and misapprehensions is to be found in the principle applied by Brandt during his studies. The purpose of the above account of the method in "The Young Søren Kierkegaard" has been to elaborate and support Vilh. Andersen's criticism.

In 1935 Brandt published a paper on "Søren Kierkegaard og Mozart's Don Juan" in the Swedish periodical "Theoria", in which he attempts

[1] The Danish word for churchyard is "Kirkegaard".

"to bring a couple of insignificant Diapsalmata under the biographical aspect." By a collation of some literary and private notes made by Søren Kierkegaard on Don Juan, Brandt tries to prove that his encounter with Don Juan was not only a profound artistic satisfaction to Kierkegaard, but that the opera had a fatal significance for him: it seized him diabolically and drove him out of the solitary monkish life of his quiet youth, filling him with a demoniacal delight in living which, however, on account of his special psychic disposition he could not satisfy in reality; hence the double note in his remarks on Mozart. He filled him with delight in living and afterwards deceived him with deprivation. The greater part of the notes used here date from the time around 1836, the time when Søren Kierkegaard went astray, and Brandt in conclusion cautiously argues that the reason why Søren Kierkegaard in 1839 can call Mozart "the murderer of my joy" perhaps is that the joy in life which the music evoked in him also drove him to the moral fall which P. A. Heiberg thought he had proved in "An Episode".

In the same year that this paper in the periodical appeared Brandt, in collaboration with Else Rammel, issued a small book "Søren Kierkegaard og Pengene" (S. K. and Money). It arose as a by-product in the tremendous process of fermentation during which "The Young Søren Kierkegaard" came into existence. It is based on a number of account books which Brandt happened to come across when writing his large book. Thus in its essence the small book is akin to the large one, aiming at the same subject, the clearing up of Kierkegaard's relation to actual bourgeois reality, and using the same means, bringing to light hitherto unheeded material which may serve as a supplement to Kierkegaard's diaries, in which the picture of the reality is subjectively misdrawn; but because of the difference of the sources the two books have after all become rather different in outward type. No problems of method are associated with the little book on Kierkegaard and Money which has been based on minute books and account books; it might have been written by an accountant; but nevertheless the book is not without significance. It answers a question which has occupied enquirers and the admirers of Søren Kierkegaard, the intellectual, ever since his death, but does not give the answer generally expected. Enquirers (i.e. Brandes, Brøchner, Troels Lund and others) had made various suggestions to explain how it was possible that Søren Kierkegaard's fortune could disappear in the course of 17 years, but in one thing they agreed, they strongly emphasised the connection between Kierkegaard's economic dispositions and his Christian persuasion. Besides for sustaining life it was thought that his money was spent on the publication of his books and in charity, and that for Old Testament reasons he would not take interest on it. Brandt shows that these statement are due, in great part, to myths and misapprehensions. Søren Kierkegaard managed his money affairs with excellent commercial talent, and he made no small sums by his writings, though not sufficient to live on, hence his complaints that he lost money by producing. He was charitable but apparently only on a small scale. The greater part of his very considerable fortune he spent on living, on housekeeping, drives, visits to restaurants etc.—The result of Brandt's very thorough enquiry into Kierkegaard's money affairs then is that in a certain way it was superfluous. Søren Kierkegaard's economic dispositions and his Christian existential doctrine do not throw any light on each other. But this negative knowledge has its importance too, it makes the traditional picture of the idealist Søren Kierkegaard fall asunder as an illusion and emphasises the necessity of remembering Søren Kierkegaard's admission that he was not a Christian himself, but still merely a poet. "Perhaps", says Brandt sagaciously on concluding his book, "some reader will think that Kierkegaard wanders out of this treatise slightly reduced. That of course depends on what he expected. We on our part must confess that one thing and another has also surprised us. But when one "recovers oneself" everything comes right again. Kierkegaard remains what he was; the fact of the matter is the simple one that his conflicts, that which made him what he was, had nothing to do with the conditions here explained. If any one has thought so it is a delusion."

Brandt's following really consists of one enquirer only, KNUD JENSENIUS, (b. 1903, secondary school teacher) whose two essential works, to make up for it, follow directly in the wake of the book on "The Young Søren Kierkegaard", both as regards method and contents. In an article on "Det unge Menneske hos Søren Kierkegaard" (The Young Person in S. K., Nordisk Tidsskrift 1930, p. 340 ff.) Jensenius attempts to prove that yet another of Søren Kierkegaard's æsthetes is drawn from a living model. The young, virginally pure, and melancholy man who appears in the symposium of the "Stages" is taken to be a portrait of Søren Kierkegaard's young friend Hans Brøchner. The wording of one of the notes in Brøchner's reminiscences: "I blushed so easily, and the sight of that always pleased him in "the young person"", and the outer and inner resemblance between "the young person" in the Stages and the classically handsome and pensive Brøchner, which may be ascertained by a comparison between Kierkegaard's description and the transmitted literary and illustrative portraits of the supposed model, constitute the evidence for the correctness of his hypothesis on which Jensenius principally relies. However, it is not compelling; only on the assumption that Brandt's arguments for Søren Kierkegard's extensive use of living models has been accepted, will the undeniably suggestive remark of Brøchner induce one to incorporate him, too, among the models; the remark in fact permits of several conjectures. And as regards the resemblance between Brøchner and the young person, the outward likeness can never acquire evidential force, because Kierkegaard's characterisation is couched in general, idealising terms, and the inner likeness is quite dispelled in the face of the resemblance between the young person and the young undergraduate Johannes Climacus in "De omnibus dubitandum est", of whom no one can think, or has ever thought, that he was drawn from Brøchner. Jensenius's article must stand and fall by the work to which it is an appendix.

His large treatise "Nogle Kierkegaard-Studier. De tre store Ideer" (Some Kierkegaard Studies. The three great Ideas; 1932) is a direct continuation of Brandt's book and therefore also of Heiberg's investigations on Søren Kierkegaard's notes from his youth concerning the three legendary figures Don Juan, Faustus, and Ahasuerus. Here he attempts, as has now become the custom, to project these three representatives of an æsthetic view of life from universal history into Kierkegaard's individual history and from this angle again to shed light on the types, so that we see their shadows in Kierkegaard's production.

Of comparatively slight importance for Kierkegaard's history is Don Juan. He belongs to that spontaneity which Kierkegaard, who began with reflection, skipped. In Faustus and Ahasuerus, on the other hand, he recognises himself; the states of mind peculiar to these two figures were prevalent in Kierkegaard's mind in the years 1836-38.—In the summer of 1835 Kierkegaard recognised himself as a modern Faustus, a man without any central point, who had innumerable interests but who was possessed of a pervading doubt which accompanied and hampered all his endeavours. This state of dissolution continued after "the earthquake" (autumn 1835), but the Faustian longing and insatiable desire to embrace everything had then acquired a strong likeness to a defiance of Christianity. However, the Faustian in Søren Kierkegaard not only manifested itself in a certain period of his life, it was part of his nature. "That which Kierkegaard understood as the Faustian in himself is not primarily aspiration, interests, even in the most Faustian form: it is something deeper, it is his very psychic faculties and disposition which amongst other things make him enter into and live with the ideas" (p. 59). These qualities may be grouped under three labels: "Imagination, absorption, and imitation" (p. 60). It is the strength especially of the first of these qualities which conditions that obliquity in Kierkegaard's mentality which he himself in The Sickness unto Death has characterised as a lack of finiteness and necessity in the synthesis of the ego. Jensenius argues that it was primarily this Faustian tendency to retire from the world and its actual tasks that Poul Møller tried to overcome in Kierkegaard, and that his influence can be observed to assert itself vigorously after his death in 1838 when Kierkegaard tried to concentrate on a limited task (the book on Hans Andersen) and approach reality, a bourgeois existence (examination, thesis, and betrothal). Kierkegaards' interest in Faustus has not left many traces in his production, but, Jensenius thinks, more than have hitherto been heeded. Both in the merman in "Fear and Trembling" and in Johannes the Seducer Faustian rudiments may be observed, in the latter they are supposed to manifest themselves in the shape of a 'deeper' layer under the surface, a yearning after spotaneity which, according to Kierkegaard's typological system, was just thought to be characteristic of Faustus, who represents Don Juan's stage in a higher intellectual sphere.—Kierkegaard's feeling of being an Ahasuerus dates from the "Earthquake" and is thus closely connected with the family tragedy. He thinks that he is cursed by God on account of his father's guilt and therefore grows indignant with Christianity, which reaction God again answers by making him a real Ahasuerus, i.e. burdening him with an inner suffering which puts him outside the common lot. This painful notion of being excluded from the common lot on account of God's anger remained in Kierkegaard's mind until his father died in 1838, and by dying at peace invalidated both the theory that he would survive his children and that he was cursed by God. "The thought of Ahasuerus disappears just because his father dies in peace; his melancholy and the secret suffering persist, but Kierkegaard fights his way to a new, Christian view of it, indicated by the expression "the thorn in the flesh"" (p. 101). This Christian clarity and understanding of the divine significance of his fundamental failing Kierkegaard did not, however, acquire immediately after his father's death; the temporary consequence was that the Ahasuerus idea was expelled. Not until 1843 could Kierkegaard adopt the Pauline expression "the thorn in the flesh" as the name for his complaint, which implies that he then understood his religious position as follows: "I am saved by God's grace, but God lets the "hidden", the disproportion, persist to remind me of my sin (it is then a kind of punishment) and at the same time I may just in this see a sign that God has a special task for me" (p. 110). Jensenius sees the literary after-effect of Kierkegaard's Ahasuerus experience in the formation of the existential category "demoniacal humour"; it is the form of life which finds its expression in æsthete A's lectures to symparanekromenoi in the Rotation Method and the Diapsalmata. Only an incomplete account can be given of Jensenius's book: it has no connected exposition of a limited subject, but consists of scattered studies which are to serve as supplements to Heiberg's, Brandt's, and Hirsch's lengthy enquiries into the history of Kierkegaard's youth. His method—that of studying the psychology of the author—coincides with that adopted by Brandt and P. A. Heiberg in their analyses of Kierkegaard's romantic æsthetic notes from his youth, and which was made the subject of criticism when we discussed Heiberg's books.

It is true, as has previously been remarked, that Brandt's following merely consisted of Jensenius, but it should be mentioned that in 1936 HANS BRIX (b. 1870, Professor of Danish Literature in the University of Copenhagen 1924-41) wrote an article on "the Earthquake" (Analyser og Problemer III. p. 288 seq.)

Among the sources used here by Brix there was an important series of articles by the biographer SEJER KÜHLE (b. 1886): Nogle Oplysninger om Søren Kierkegaard (Some Information about Søren Kierkegaard) 1834-38, (Personalhistorisk Tidsskr. 1931-35). In these articles there are few arguments or conclusions, but a number of facts, so far unheeded or partly unknown, are cleared up with precision. This applies for instance to the quarrels in the Kierkegaard family, which are elucidated by extracts from P. C. Kierkegaard's diaries, and a church list of the occasions when members of the family attended Holy Communion. Together with a list of the cases of sickness and death occurring in the family in the years 1830-35 they formed the basis of a reconstruction of that family crisis which Kierkegaard later retained in his memory under the symbol of "The Earthquake".

Brix tries to fill in the gaps in Kierkegaard's diaries with second-hand information; but it should be emphasised that Brix's historical method does not in any way remind one of Brandt's. Brix understands the "Earthquake" notes "as an expression of a plan Kierkegaard had of writing the history of his life in novel form" and thus looks at them from a literary point of view. His interpretation is to the effect that in the autumn of 1835 when the eldest son Peter Christian Kierkegaard was attacked by a severe illness Kierkegaard and his father talked together about the frequent deaths in the family and surpassed each other in melancholy imaginings. The fact that Søren Kierkegaard's other brothers and sisters had died before they were 34 years old they connected with the father's puerile cursing of God and inferred that it was the Lord's intention that none of the hosier's children should survive their 33rd year. On Søren Kierkegaard who returned from his holiday with his head full of future plans this discovery must have acted as an earthquake, and he was overcome with despair. That this new interpretation of the over-interpreted document is in the main correct appears from a letter Kierkegaard wrote to his brother on his birthday on the 5th May 1847, in which he expresses his great surprise at having attained the age of 34. "Both father and I had the idea that none in our family would live to be more than 34 years old." This strange notion Kierkegaard allowed to influence his work, Brix thinks, and surely not without justice; "On account of it he had beforehand arranged for an effective termination to his literary production, namely with "Concluding Unscientific Postcript" and the added "Explanation of his Authorship". They appeared in 1846 before his decease, which may be expected at any moment after the 5th May this year" (p. 301).—That Brix's interpretation of "the Earthquake" is in the main correct can hardly be disputed—in spite of Rubow's assurance that "no mortal can judge of the secret events in Kierkegaard's biography" (Tendencies p. 161). It is based exclusively on notes and letters in which Kierkegaard and his relatives use direct speech, and is thus unique in the history of Kierkegaard research.

C. *"Biological" Psychology*

In a small treatise, "Fortolkninger til Søren Kierkegaards Ungdomshistorie" (Interpretations of Søren Kierkegaard's Early History). (Publications of the Royal Norwegian Society of Sciences 1925, No. 4 pp. 1-32) JOHS. D. LANDMARK (1876-1938, librarian) has tried to arrive at a more precise determination of the time and content of the "Earthquake". In contrast with P. A. Heiberg whose methods and results he otherwise adopts, and in agreement with Ellekilde, Landmark contends that the "earthquake" was due to a definite external event. It must have taken place in the period between the 4th August and the 14th September 1835 and have consisted in Søren Kierkegaard accidentally learning that his father had committed the sin against the Holy Ghost. Not until 1837 did he learn in what the sin consisted. It will be seen that Landmark chiefly tries to verify the hypothesis advanced by Heiberg and Ellekilde that in the autumn of 1835 Kierkegaard only suspected the facts of the "earthquake" in his father's life and did not come to know them until 1837. The most interesting point about Landmark's treatise is not, however, his attempts to improve upon the results brought to light by reflective psychology, but the fact that towards the close of his work he has a statement which, rightly understood, is a blow to the whole of this trend within Kierkegaard research: "On the 19th May we have the testimony to that transition to joy which, psychologically, is so remarkable to us, because it shows a decided change of feeling.—Kierkegaard himself did not later in life understand the inner forces here active in his mind. Least of all did he regard his own experience as a revelation from a supersensual world. Against this he emphatically protests. His father's death was of more decisive importance to him than the awakening of his own feelings. In this connection we may ask whether he actually understood what was the significant point about the "earthquake". Would not Kierkegaard's development in his youth have taken the same course for inner reasons if he had not surprised his father in his contrition, as told in Solomon's Dream? Did not Kierkegaard in the autumn of 1835 enter upon a long period of depression quite independent of external events? It may well be conceived that the "earthquake" gained its greatest significance precisely because it occurred just at the time when it was bound to exert a quite special effect on an impressionable mind" (p. 28).—In an article 8 years later entitled "Periander and Kierkegaard's Love Story" (Nordisk Tidskrift 1933) Landmark attempts to consider the history of Kierkegaard's engagement from this wider psychological angle that he himself recommended in the remark quoted above. Starting from the fifth of the ill-starred insertions, "Periander, the lesson by book", Landmark proceeds to philosophise on the strange circumstances of Kierkegaard's betrothal. He arrives at the result that if Kierkegaard could become engaged in 1840 and write in his diary in 1843, "If I had had faith I should have stayed with Regine", then the obstacles which in the meantime had necessitated a breach cannot have been decisive. The resistance to marriage must have had its root in some inner state of mind in Søren Kierkegaard and can only have been casually founded on an objective fact. And what sort of inner state this was Landmark claims that he can infer from "Periander". For this is the tale of a tyrannical father and a defiant son. And the father exterminates himself by a self-appointed assassination. If we identify Periander and his son with the old hosier and his son, and consider that the latter wrote the story, then it seems to testify that Søren Kierkegaard suffered from an Oedipus complex. "If we trace Kierkegaard's view of the father as a tyrant back to its earliest stage we shall finally find its earliest antecedent in the physiological attitude of the baby turned from the more remote figure of the father towards the protection of the mother organism" (p. 23). This then is Landmark's psycho-analytical hypothesis, that Kierkegaard's whole behaviour during his engagement was subconsciously regulated by a physiological aversion to marriage. Though the mother complex was subdued, and the memory of the father sacred to him, it is conceivable that his original feeling for his mother was still present as a rudiment in his adult personality and forced him to actions for which he was only able to give sham reasons because the real motives were buried in his subconsciousness.—It would seem superfluous to go more closely into this theory; Landmark has no right to identify the hosier and Periander, Kierkegaard and Lycophron etc. (on the insertions cf. above). And even though psycho-analysts have always understood how to manage with very little, the fact that Søren Kierkegaard loved his father and never mentioned his mother must, I think, be said to be too slender a foundation for the conjecture that he suffered from an Oedipus complex. But the two articles have not been reviewed so much for their own sake as because they at the same time mark the breach with the narrow psychological school whose field of work is bounded by Kierkegaard's mind, and form a transition from Heiberg's trend in Kierkegaard research to the new school whose first representative Helweg is. Landmark literally points to him in the last lines of his second article: "The treatment of the whole subject of Kierkegaard has in our day advanced to the point when we cannot in the central questions acquire any further essential insight solely by means of the text-critical method and literary psychological procedure. Research will only reach its final stage when the biographical material, as it can now be arranged, is closely examined by a many-sided medical-psychiatric authority" (p. 32).

Hjalmar Helweg (b. 1886) is one of the most important and most influential of Danish psychiatrists. In 1919 he was appointed chief physician of the Mental Hospital of Oringe and in 1937 appointed professor in the University of Copenhagen and chief physician of the Rigshospital. In addition to this exacting work he has, as a forensic psychiatrist, made a comprehensive theoretical and practical contribution which is regarded as pioneer work. And finally he has contributed to Danish literary biography by studies of N. F. S. Grundtvig, Hans Andersen, and Søren Kierkegaard, dealing with the latter in the large volume "Søren Kierkegaard. En psykiatrisk-psykologisk studie" (1933).

These contributions to literary history all belong to the pathographical kind, which practically, though not etymologically, consist in psychiatrical interpretations of the mind and fate of historical men of merit. This genre belongs to the mazy field between the natural sciences and the humanities, where the clinical judgment of the psychiatrist meets and wrestles with the psychological intuition of the historian.—Pathographical works evade criticism by the uninitiated, and uninitiated are, according to the experts, not only the critics who lack essential knowledge of the science of psychiatry, but any one who has not many years' experience as an alienist. This assertion partly disarms the æsthete but it does not prevent him from grumbling.

That in spite of all it only partly disarms him is due to the fact that, when the æsthete and the psychiatrist study the same material, the same text may seem to have a different structure to the different eyes reading it; if the two views exclude each other there is no reason why the æsthete should resign. A more important reason, however, is that at a certain point the investigation of the psychiatrist always comes into the common daylight and from that moment must be accessible to non-psychiatrical criticism. The pathographical investigation always describes a double movement, from the complex mind or work to the diagnosis, the indication of the active psychic forces and their combination; and from the recognition of the general character of the disease to the explanation of what is individual. As to the correctness of the first movement one must, as an outsider, refrain from giving any opinion, of the second movement it may be briefly said that it cannot be carried out, though many allow themselves to be deceived. The circumstance that a recognised psychic factor, e.g. a depression, manifests itself in a poet's actions or work neither explains his actions nor his work, in so far as it is the individual realisation that is of interest.

Thus when Mogens Ellermann in his book "Genius and Insanity" shows that schizophrenia slowly transformed and broke down Ernst Josephson's creative pictorial talent, the illustrative documentation of the growth of the disease is absolutely convincing; the healthy painter's free and sure talent, the broken down painter's morbid and valueless perseveration, and between them the afflicted but not ruined artist's painfully original production in the period of conflict. With justice Ellerman explains the artistic revival in the time just before the collapse as the insanity increasing, or altering, the talent before it burns it out. But how flimsy is the contribution to the understanding of the individual drawings or of the artist's intention with them which he can extract from this observation. "In the interesting work "The Creation of Adam", which has not without reason been most discussed and admired, there is, besides the misdrawing, something peculiar in the linework and the subject itself which is undoubtedly due to the schizophrenic process. Josephson would hardly, had he remained sane, have strayed to these fields, so different from those in which his previous art found its soil" (pp. 45-46).

But thus it must be. Of the name and form of the insanity and its general effect, of what it checks and arrests, the physician can inform us but of what it produces in conjunction with genius or merely ordinary intelligence, of this the physician, as physician, cannot tell us anything. Every one must make the transition from the general picture of the disease to the actual work by the aid of the amount of psychological intuition which has been given to him. Therefore the knowledge we can obtain through these pathographical works is not without interest, but it is rather useless for historical or æsthetic purposes. The ring of cognition cannot be broken, but it may well work magic.

In his book on Søren Kierkegaard Helweg advances the opinion that he suffered from a manic-depressive psychosis of endogenous origin which set in in the year 1835 and persisted till his death. The nature and course of his severe attacks of melancholy, his self-accusations and sensations of fear, speak decisively in favour of this. And the correctness of the diagnosis is strengthened by the fact that this mental disease was found in Kierkegaard's family and seems to have been inherited directly from parents to children. To all appearance his father suffered from it, and so quite undoubtedly did his brother Peter and the son of the latter. And Søren Kierkegaard, as we see, did not escape; but in him the disease did not take the usual course—which, indeed, could not be expected. According to Kretschmer's doctrine of constitutions the pure forms of manic-depressive psychosis occur almost exclusively in persons whose build is pycnic, and whose nature is syntonic, and none of these terms can be applied to Kierkegaard without reserve. According to the pictures that have come down to us he approximated physically to the asthenic type, but, Helweg points out, illness and an altogether delicate constitution may have obliterated pycnic traits if such had been present. And as regards Kierkegaard's psychic constitution Helweg thinks that in spite of the pseudonymity, the indirect communication, and the idealistic fanaticism which point towards schizoid dispositions—we shall find as the central factor of Søren Kierkegaard's nature "extroverted affectivity, desire for human contacts, sympathy and a faculty of feeling with others in their sufferings" (p. 358), i.e. purely syntonic elements. But the depression that forced him to use violence against himself led him into austerity and isolation which were foreign to his original nature. All in all, however, it must be said that constitutionally Kierkegaard was an alloy, and therefore the inherited manic-depressive psychosis in him took an atypical course. An examination of his diaries and books shows that the disease manifested itself in long fluctuations of mood; now and then there occurred manic exaltation like flashes as e.g. on the 19th May 1838 and the 19th April 1848, most frequently the mixed state with a depressive mood and manic form of reaction in which he was in the period when he wrote his pseudonymous literature. On a few occasions he was tormented by such violent depressions that his will-power was quite paralysed and he stopped thinking; this happened e.g. in the months around the turn of the year 1837-38 and in June-July 1848.—A complete account of Helweg's exposition of the varying ebb and flow in the tides of Kierkegaard's soul is not intended here; that would involve unnecessary repetition of our preceding statements, and the description of the course of the phychosis is to Helweg only the means to the end of explaining the effects of the disease on Kierkegaard's life and production, how it determined his actions and ideas in the individual cases. In the sequel therefore the account of Helweg's book will be concentrated on his contribution to the solution of the classical problems.

Since research on Kierkegaard's history was started enquirers have again and again wondered at the disproportionateness of his reactions. The crises of his life, as far as can be judged, were caused by incidents which normal persons would confine themselves to regretting. From this circumstance Heiberg and Geismar have drawn each his own conclusion of the two that are possible, that Kierkegaard was morbidly sensitive, or that we lack sufficient knowledge of the decisive events of his life. Helweg, however, declares that none of them is right, their presentation of the problem is wrong. It is true that the sudden upsets in Kierkegaard's life are insufficiently explained in his diaries, but the explanation of that is not that he has kept back a "secret note", but that he himself did not know the true causes of the catastrophe, the slowly developing depressions of endogenous origin, and therefore was bound to ascribe them to sad events, unfortunate circumstances, as the causes. Thus when Kierkegaard returned from Gilleleje in the summer of 1835 determined to build up a glorious future, he suffered the first outbreak of depression in his life, it extinguished the light in him, and forced him to give up his good intentions. "Then it was that the great earthquake occurred——", he writes later on and casts the blame on his discovery of his father's early guilt, but at the time when he made the discovery he can hardly have attached any great importance to it. "More probably it must be supposed that the famous word was spoken in 1835 when Kierkegaard came home and found his father in psychic disintegration, but that it was only later when Søren Kierkegaard's own state of mind changed, when his own feelings were harrowed by agitation, that it exerted its influence and appeared to him as the point of departure, as the "earthquake" (p. 66).—In a quite similar manner the history of his engagement must be interpreted. When Kierkegaard returned from his pilgrimage to Sæding he was firmly resolved to have Regine, made tempestuous love to her and was accepted. Then again a strong depression set in and forced him to retreat, and gradually it seemed to him that the engagement was rendered impossible by his past history, by his and his father's closely connected sins. "But all this was only deliberations, formations he built up from the material given him in the conflict between the strong currents of feeling. The healthy love collided with the morbid depression and at the first decisive meeting suffered defeat, it could not break through, the insect died at the moment of fecundation" (p. 147).

While thus the depressions have an inhibiting influence on Kierkegaard, forcing him to break his plighted word, the brief periods of exaltation, as might be duly expected, have the opposite effect, helping him to realise intentions which were on the point of being sicklied o'er with the pale cast of thought. The sudden delight he experiences on the 19th May at half past ten in the morning must, if we go to the depths, be regarded as an endogenous oscillation of mood in a positive direction. It is no revelation, no transcendental new departure, as maintained by Heiberg, but merely an experience of an "intense feeling of joy, which seems like a refreshing and cooling breeze after the crushing depression" (p. 118); nevertheless the event becomes of religious significance to Kierkegaard by the fact that the trend of his mind towards religion is now given free play" (120). "In this lies the factor, eminently peculiar to Kierkegaard, that the direction and especially the speed of his thoughts are presumably to a great extent conditioned by the endogenous fluctuations of mood, but that nevertheless he always, whether or not he is conscious of the nature of these changes at the moment, can retain and take his stand on the thoughts which are thus set in motion. But if we want to get to the bottom of his religious awakening in May 1838 it is no good tracing his train of thought up to that point and disregarding the change of mood underlying it, which alone made it possible for his thoughts to speed on in the direction in which they were aimed. And the subjectively intense Christianity, actually undogmatic, which later became peculiar to Kierkegaard, probably has its deepest explanation in the circumstance that his movement towards Christianity is set in motion and sustained by an inexplicable, unreasoned, indescribable joy, by a sudden lifting of his depression" (p. 120). From these lines appears the significance for Søren Kierkegaard's religious awakening, and his Christian views altogether, which Helweg claims must be ascribed to that state of sudden joy which on the 19th May arose in Kierkegaard's mind from organic causes. It turns out that the depressions, however much they may arrest his outward activities, may have a furthering influence on his personal engrossment in and absorption of Christianity. When in 1849 he had set up the ideal demand of Christianity in its consistent unattainableness he had to hide behind a pen-name—recognising that he had reached the bounds of his individuality—i.e. for his own person he had to admit the impossibility of uniting life and doctrine. "In reality the logical consequence of his own thought would seem to be a dissociation from Christianity" (p. 258). But Søren Kierkegaard keeps to Christianity in spite of logic, and Helweg thinks it is his morbid melancholy which makes this decision in defiance of reason. "There is something which pricks him on to cross the narrow line between despair-to-madness and Christianity. And this something was the basic depressive mood instinct with the idea of sin engendered by fear. He must have a point to hold on to" (p. 258). This keeping to Christianity combined with the introduction of the pseudonym Anti-Climacus, P. A. Heiberg regards as the splendid result of Kierkegaard's offensive against his melancholy, which on this occasion was nearly exterminated. Helweg, on the other hand, contends that his melancholy lasted till his death; but in 1849 there occurred the change that he came to understand what he could endure and what not. "Through this he does not achieve a recovery from the attacks of depression, for they still come, but he achieves what he himself had seen was the maximum of the attainable, that he can endure them. He no longer revolted against them, but respected them as the determining factor in his soul life that they had always been" (p. 273). —Concluding this survey we must finally mention Helweg's psychiatrical explanation of Kierkegaard's last aggression. Ever since Kierkegaard's death it had been a general wish that a psychiatrist should express his scientifically founded opinion of "The Moment". Most briefly expressed Helweg's opinion is that the views Kierkegaard advocates in „The Moment" have come into being in the same way as those of the fox about the grapes. "It is this turning in unrestrained exasperation against that which is desired in vain which characterises Kierkegaard's state of mind during his onslaught on the Church" (p. 258). Morbidness forced the idea on him that it was his Christian duty to die from this world, and this caused an inner tumult ending in his condemning "the beautiful humanity which not long before he had declared his love". His attack on marriage, the clergy, the Church, was thus actually Kierkegaard's last desperate settlement with himself. And the ruthless brutal form of the pamphlets was again due to his disease. "Søren Kierkegaard was in a pathological state which in no small degree suspended his sound judgment" (p. 282). However, "there are no grounds for regarding this last eruption of Kierkegaard's soul life as a regular attack of disease.— — —It was a psychologically understandable final stage of a psychic development, which behind the rich trains of thought was dynamically determined by the basic affective elements, the depressive and the manic. It may thus be said that the assault on the Church was not in the proper sense a manifestation of the manic-depressive psychosis from which Kierkegaard suffered, but the psychological consequence of its effect on his mind and his development" (pp. 304-305).

As previously stated, it is not possible for a layman to decide whether the peculiarities of Kierkegaard's soul which Helweg has observed and described are sufficient in number and pregnancy to justify scientifically the assertion that Kierkegaard suffered from a manic-depressive psychosis. Some of the features of Kierkegaard's person and production which Helweg adduces in support of his diagnosis have been differently explained by others, wholly or partly experts. Of those symptoms of manic-depressive psychosis which Helweg claims to have observed in Kierkegaard he especially stresses that Kierkegaard suffered from fear. That he did so is supposed to appear from his book "The Concept of Dread", about which it is claimed that he wrote it on the basis of the sinister experiences he had in the time before and after the lapse of 1836. Helweg concludes his analysis of the book as follows: "And thus we have learnt through this speculative work that the whole period was characterised by dread, first a sinister mysterious dread not of anything definite, without any object and inexplicable, but depriving him of all firm holds and thus drawing him towards the abyss; and later a dread, if possible still deeper, binds his thought to the catastrophe of sin, forces it to close around the fearful, and seems to bar every way out. It is, I think, difficult to get nearer to the feeling of dread in the typical depression" (p. 90). In his attractive little book "Angst-Begrebet i Søren Kierkegaard: Begrebet Angst" (The Dread Concept of Søren Kierkegaard: The Concept of Dread) IB OSTENFELD (b. 1902, M.D.) expresses another opinion (not for the purpose of refuting Helweg; the two alienists' publications appeared in the same year, 1933). An analysis of Kierkegaard's work leads him to the view that dread, as there described, is not quite identical with what is generally meant by dread, but an expression of the constant longing for peace and redemption which stirs all creation. "There is then in Søren Kierkegaard's use of this term in itself nothing to justify the assumption of a concrete feeling of dread as a personal experience in Søren Kierkegaard (p. 87). If therefore we wish to relate the dread to Kierkegaard's person the only permissible question is what special garb this longing and unrest assumed for Kierkegaard himself. Ostenfeld claims that it may with a fair degree of certainty be inferred that Søren Kierkegaard, in his description of the demoniacal, i.e. the dread of the good, has given a veiled autobiography. And the dread in the demoniacal he understands as an obscure pain at the back of the mind which may be co-ordinated with Pascal's feeling of always having an abyss at his left side, a chronic unhappy state of mind, half intellectually, half emotionally determined. "In Kierkegaard the "abyss" must have been the persistent vital feeling of insecurity in his relation to his fellow beings. With this must have been combined an instinctive propensity to fix his attention on all that was coloured by distaste in life, all that may have a depressing, undermining, disillusioning effect (pp. 109-10). If this is the case, we may dismiss the thought of identifying Kierkegaard's dread with the well-known pathological form of dread, Ostenfeld thinks; his explanation of the disagreement between Kierkegaard's dread and the depressive affect of dread is of special interest in this connection. "Kierkegaard's dread is not, like this (the depressive dread), accompanied by inhibition of the mental functions. On the contrary, the dread seems rather to animate his thinking and urge it on to unusual effort. The dread of the melancholic forms a strong contrast to what has been said here. He, as no one else, experiences his dread as a manifest reality which forces him into self-abandonment and a complete feeling of impotence. All thoughts seem to have stopped dead in him, and he is seized with a feeling of inner emptiness. Out of this state wrong notions of his own guilt and eternal perdition will then necessarily spring. The whole picture is saturated with gloom and deep anxiety" (p. 100). There is reason to trust the result of Ostenfeld's detailed study. In contrast with Helweg, to whom the dogmatic-speculative reflections in "The Concept of Dread" are merely an obstacle to the psychological understanding, and who goes to the reading of the book in the hope of finding the depressive feeling of dread as the personal core of the treatise, Ostenfeld understands the book as a literary whole, before he begins his psychological analysis of the author, which is a cautious procedure, and he carries it through consistently for the sake of the analysis itself, without being constrained by any theory. Hence it may be said with a probability verging on certainty that Kierkegaard was not harrowed by such fits of dread as are typical of the constitutional melancholic, or at least that the book in which Helweg finds them described deals with something else. If this is so, then, according to Helweg's own view one of his chief proofs that Kierkegaard suffered from a manic-depressive psychosis would fall away. "Dread is so essential an element of the typical manic-depressive psychosis that one would almost hesitate to make this diagnosis, if the dread were not present" (Helweg p. 84).—In other quarters too the correctness of Helweg's diagnosis has been disputed. According to the theories developed by Kretschmer in "Körperbau und Character" there is a close relation between a particular psycho-physical type of constitution and the manic-depressive psychosis. This theory, Helweg says, does not mean "that the manic-depressive psychosis is excluded where the respective physical and psychic types cannot be demonstrated, or at least do not appear clearly, but nevertheless the interdependence goes so far that the pure constitutional forms and the manic-depressive cases appearing in their typical form coincide in an absolutely predominant degree, while a more atypical, mixed constitution, a constitutional alloy, is as a rule associated with a less typical course of the disease" (p. 336). It must be permissible to conclude from this that if, psychically and physically, Søren Kierkegaard was of the lean type, it is improbable that he should have harboured a manic-depressive psychosis. It is at this point that the Swedish psychologist JOHN BJÖRKHEM (b. 1910) has come forward. The main part of his little book "Søren Kierkegaard i psykologisk belysning" (Søren Kierkegaard in a Psychological Light; 1942), which is actually a counter-argument to Helweg's treatise, is devoted to proving that Kierkegaard belonged to the asthenic-schizothymic constitutional type. Without sarcasm Björkhem passes over Helweg's somewhat forced attempt to demonstrate pycnic features in Kierkegaard's physique: he concentrates on proving that in mind and temper Kierkegard was schizothymic. His documentation occupies more than half the book and is divided into five sections; here we shall only give the main arguments by which he supports his contention. Søren Kierkegaard experienced "the world more powerfully in thought and imagination than in external contact through action". He had an inclination to hide his own self at any cost; he kept to his habits with a precision that verged on pedantry; he preferred intercourse with ideas rather than with men, he followed up the development of his thoughts with inexorable consistency, had an unprecedented feeling of responsibility, could not rid himself of a strong impression once received; he was onesided, reactionary, fanatical, and radical. These are all features characteristic of the schizothymic personality—and their number could be doubled without difficulty. But it is not the circumstance that in great and small things a considerable number of similarities may be pointed out between Kierkegaard and the schizothymic nature which constitutes the final proof of the correctness of Björkhem's view. More important as a criterion is the fact that on the assumption of a schizotymic disposition in Kierkegaard, his peculiarities in relation to his fellow beings and the peculiarities of his writings may without constraint be explained, unaided by the hypothesis that he was insane. And that this hypothesis is very little probable Björkhem thinks can be proved primarily by reference to the facts that Kierkegaard never acted without a motive, but constantly preserved his self-control, and that in his poetic treatment of personal problems he only describes psychic experiences and events which any person who lives intensely will recognise from himself.

Whether these arguments adduced by a semi-competent person (Björkhem when he wrote the book had no clinical experience) and which strongly impress an incompetent person, are of sufficient weight to affect Helweg's diagnosis must be left open. That Kierkegaard's contemporaries and posterity have fixed their attention less on his "extroverted affectivity" and capacity for human sympathy than on his labyrinthine nature and uncanny ability to let offences breed in secret, is well known. It is of this traditional picture that Björkhem has tried to determine the type.

In his attempt to determine Kierkegaard's type of constitution and the nature of his disease Helweg introduced new problems into Kierkegaard research. His purpose was, however, the opposite one of laying a foundation for the final solution of the problems which had occupied enquirers from 1877 when the study of Kierkegaard was started, and which since 1909 had been systematically treated. Helweg did not intend to break away from the personal-historical school of Kierkegaard research, but to infuse fresh blood into it by reforming its psychological principles in general, and its causal theory in particular. Hitherto it had been thought that the causes of the abrupt changes in Kierkegaard's mood and view of life, of his fall and restoration, were to be found among the experiences and events of his life, and that accordingly he himself, if not others, knew them; therefore his papers and publications were turned topsy-turvy and all sorts of tricks were used to lure or wrest information from them concerning their author's private life. In opposition to this Helweg maintains that it is an untenable assumption that Kierkegaard should have been conscious of the real causes of the crises and conflicts of his life. The waves in his moods did not arise as a result of outer storms, but grew out of his own organism; he did not know this himself. Therefore, when some biological process caused a melancholy mood in him, and the melancholy again forced him to break his promises or give up his purposes, then these negative actions were mysterious to himself. He then searched his memory for the motives for his own conduct, and thought he found them when he remembered sad discoveries or occurrences which had taken place at about the same time as his despondency began, that is to say, he found what in psychiatry is called the depressive idea. It is these ideas that previous enquirers—deceived by the deceived author—have with difficulty traced and attached importance to as causes.

Hence Kierkegaard was not in a philosophical sense capable of making decisions, he was determined by his disease, his viscera gave the orders which his conscious person merely had to obey. The endogenous fluctuations of mood determined the rhythm of his life. It is, Helweg thinks, only partly right, for Kierkegaard's unique power of reflection was independent of the psychosis. "Each fluctuation of mood that asserts itself is taken up, elaborated and used, an attempt is made to work it up or subdue it according as it is found useful or injurious, and in this way the curve of his mood undoubtedly undergoes certain, perhaps at times very considerable, changes. If Kierkegaard had not had his unique reflection the curve of his moods would no doubt have had a different appearance. He depresses and modifies it with all his might. But nevertheless he cannot eliminate his pathological affective fluctuations. Under the mighty layer of his reflection the curve of the affects moves with greater or smaller oscillations and even though many times in his life, in spite of the blows these oscillations give him, he keeps hold of the trend of his thought, it happens to him more than once that the blows are so hard that they have a determining effect.—The points are shifted and he changes his direction" (p. 124). Thus Kierkegaard's psychological situation was dialectic. He was both sick and sound; as sick he was determined, as sound undetermined. When he was one thing, and when the other, is difficult too say, for, as Helweg exclaims in another passage, "what is sound and what is sick in a manic-depressive constitution? A foundation of paradigmatic soundness mingles intimately with the influence of pathological fluctuations of mood— —" (p. 214). In his forensic psychology he answers the question as follows: "It cannot in the individual case of an insane person be established where the sickness stops and where normal thought begins." As will appear from the above-cited explanation of the relation between the endogenous affective oscillation and the reflection, it may, however, in Kierkegaard's case be established that in certain periods the unsound, determining layer in his mind had the priority. The biological compulsion was sometimes so strong that his reflection was powerless. This was the case, inter alia, at the "earthquake" and the breaking off of his engagement, when his behaviour and ideas were evidently decided by his depression. That Helweg in spite of the dialectics of the situation can have so sure an understanding of the inward meaning of these events is due to the fact that he is what Johannes Climacus calls a backward-looking prophet, i.e. a historian who allows himself to be deceived by the circumstance that the past seems more necessary than the future. And, as previously remarked, it is in reality only something he imagines when he claims that he can explain a concrete individual action by means of knowledge of the abstract nature and general effect of the depressions. If for instance Kierkegaard in 1841, instead of breaking his promise to Regine, had burnt his thesis for the doctorate, this action too might afterwards have been regarded as a necessary consequence of the depression, and so would any of the numerous possible decisions he might have made during the depression. Confronted with the fact that Kierkegaard, at a certain juncture, makes a sudden change in his external and internal affairs, Helweg as a psychiatrist is at most able to show that Kierkegaard's behaviour has the character of insanity, i.e. to describe the movement from the individual to the general, make the diagnosis once more, but nothing else; why Kierkegaard does just what he does, changing his views and plans precisely in such a distinctive and alarming way as is the case, Helweg can only explain, because it is so much easier "to understand that something has come to be after it has come to be than before it has come to be."

Besides for explaining the course of and especially the crises in Kierkegaard's life, Helweg also tries to turn the experience gained to account for a description of Kierkegaard's working process. Thus, of the psychological conditions under which the pseudonymous works were composed he writes: "Kierkegaard's thought cannot be said to be determined by the endogenous fluctuations. These do not so much decide what he is thinking of as how he is thinking it. The depressions have contributed essentially to create the material, and the hypomanic mood conditions its use, but over these factors there is a third mighty factor, the psychic quality itself which enables the individual to work with the given material, to think. This quality Søren Kierkegaard possessed in an extraordinary degree, and about this psychiatry cannot teach us anything" (p. 199). On the basis of these lines it is rather difficult to form any clear idea of what part the three psychic elements: depression, mania, and reflection, have had in Kierkegaard's writings; and the more one thinks of it the more difficult it becomes. A few pages further on Helweg has expressed his thought more precisely: "In the depressive inclination to make existential hitches the problems were created; by reflection, thought, which was itself passion, they were elaborated and solved, and by writing them down under irresistable high pressure, liberation was attained. Thus Søren Kierkegaard—by simultaneously using his positive psychic qualities and his pathological constitutional elements—found his modus vivendi" (p. 202). But this passage too is not easy. One is accustomed to regard the mind as a whole, and one does not really understand how there can be any question of a division of work, and if this is the case, and the depression and the mania have become separated from thought, one does not understand what it means that thought "itself is passion".—Presumably this brief formulation is to be regarded as a very rough analytical and poetical description of a psychic process in the real course of which it is not thought possible to separate the elements; but it must presumably be questionable how great is the value of such an approximation, when one cannot, or at any rate only on the first hasty reading, connect any ideas with it.

As a supplement to this chapter on the biological compulsion to which Søren Kierkegaard was subject may be added a discussion of the last attempt for the time being to explain Kierkegaard's melancholy and painful history, by the sculptor RICHARD MAGNUSSEN (1880-1948). In a large book of 300 pages "Søren Kierkegaard set udefra" (S. K. viewed from without, 1942) he argues that Kierkegaard was a hunchback, and in another book of 200 pages he tries to show the influence the physical deformity must have had on Kierkegaard's psychic structure. Only the first volume of the work deserves serious attention.—By a close analysis of the traditions in illustration and literature of Kierkegaard's appearance Magnussen succeeds in convincing his readers of the correctness of his fundamental thesis that Kierkegaard's physical defects were more marked than previously supposed, and that his own word "en Vanheldet" may justly be applied to himself. Whether he was actually a hunchback is a matter of controversy, and was the subject of a lively debate in the press when Magnussen's book appeared. Brandt thinks that Sibbern's subtle and well-considered formulation of his conception of Kierkegaard's exterior is the most reliable. It runs as follows: "He (S. K.) had a witty, somewhat sarcastic face, a brisk gait, was lean and not tall, with a wryness as if a slight hunch had been on the point of coming, and also had that inclination to jeer, but coupled with wit and humour, that such persons generally have" (R. M. p. 125). This statement is indeed reliable, partly because it is derived from Sibbern who knew Kierkegaard so well, partly because it is formulated after reflection. When Magnussen, in spite of Sibbern and others of Kierkegaard's contemporaries who have remarked that his back was not quite as backs ought to be, maintains that Kierkegaard was simply a hunchback, his criticism of the sources is based on the view, of course not quite unwarranted, that the physical defects of a deceased person will be described by his friends and wellwishers as charitably as possible, but it is a theory which is better suited to explain away the exception than the rule—and it is the rule to describe Kierkegaard as round-backed, crook-backed, humpbacked, high-shouldered etc.—In "Det særlige Kors" (The special Cross; 1943), the postcript, "which in so far could well—after the obvious pattern —be designated as concluding and unscientific, because the results have been predominantly arrived at in an intuitive way" (Introduction), Magnussen tries to prove that "the melancholy had perhaps its deepest cause, explaining the later development, in the purely physical, namely in the fact that Kierkegaard from his earliest youth was physically deformed" (p. 11), "that behind that lack of spontaneity that Kierkegaard admits, and that Helweg ingeniously shows to be imperfectly motivated in a psychological respect, and behind every inhibition of spontaneity on the part of the melancholy, the exhausting brooding over himself, and later the affection of the mind, there lies a far deeper, a far more sombre unspeakable feeling of defect, the deformed person's confinement to himself" (p. 77). The investigation is, however, rendered difficult by the circumstance that Kierkegaard never anywhere bluntly mentions his physical deformity, because like deformed people in general he cannot speak of his misery, but hides it in profound reserve. Nevertheless we find in Kierkegaard's papers information of his deformity and its effects on his mind "for describe his calamity he must, to give vent to it"—but it is hidden in metaphors and apparently impersonal notes. If only one reads Kierkegaard's notes in the right spirit it will appear that in countless instances he has had his deformity in mind when he wrote them. And as a matter of fact, it appears plainly to Magnussen to whom Kierkegaard's hump protrudes from every other note. Space cannot be spared here for a more detailed account or a thorough criticism of Magnussen's book, not to speak of his individual readings: there can hardly be any doubt that his documentation of the fact that Kierkegaard's exterior was so strikingly ugly that he could be said, or at least could almost be said, to be deformed, may be of a certain importance for later biographical research, and especially that Kierkegaard's disproportionate indignation at the caricatures of the Corsair will be easier to understand. But in Magnussen's own interpretation of his discovery, according to which the hump, or his grief because of the hump, was even the secret of Kierkegaard's life, the cause of his melancholy and his exceptional position, there is a farcial disproportion between his premises and his conclusions.

3. Søren Kierkegaard as a Thinker. Philosophical Theological Research

In his "Tider og Typer" (Ages and Types) Vilh. Andersen writes: "For any one who wants to penetrate into Kierkegaard's soul there are two ways to go, all according to the place where you stand yourself. You can, if you are able to do so, begin where he ended, with Christ, or where he began: with Socrates and the Greeks" (Goethe II, p. 70). This indicates the two ports of entry to Søren Kierkegaard's mentality, by which enquirers not only could have, but also really have entered. Socrates and Christ, they are his teachers in the humanities and the subject of his faith, his relation to them has determined the form and content of his writings and his attitude towards the intellectual movements of his age. Kierkegaard's thinking must therefore be understood and evaluated in the light of his faith or against the background of the humanism which arose in Hellas.

A. Søren Kierkegaard and the Humanistic Tradition

The continuation of the passage just quoted concerning the ports of entry to Kierkegaard's mentality is the first detailed treatment of his indebtedness to the tradition of the ancients. It forms part of an exposition of the history of classical culture in Denmark, which appeared in two double volumes: Erasmus 1-2 (1907-09) and Goethe 1-2 (1915-16). In this work and in his illustrated History of Danish Literature (III 1924 pp. 679-706) VILHELM ANDERSEN (b. 1864; Professor in the University of Copenhagen 1908-30) has written about Søren Kierkegaard, i.e. when a general historical survey made it necessary. Of a personal inducement there has hardly been any question; in his comprehensive and fundamental works on the history of literature he shows sympathy with the harmonious, and understanding of the divided types of mentality, but feels alien to pathological and frozen minds.

Here we shall only discuss in more detail his account of Kierkegaard's relation to the Greeks. It occurs in the second half volume of the book on Goethe (pp. 65-108). Vilh. Andersen has here marked off the Greek period in Kierkegaard's individual history and pointed out partly the nature of the Greek influence on his thought, partly the psychological factors conditioning his transition from the rhetorical (Goethean-Hegelian) to the personal (Socratic-Platonic) humanism, and his later radical rupture with humanism in favour of Christianity.—The transition to the Socratic stage in Kierkegaard's development is dated by Vilh. Andersen at 1837. Until then his type had been Faustus, the doubting and seeking spirit of extroverted intellectualism, which finds its expression in the poetry and philosophy of romanticism; but then, like Plato by Socrates, he let himself be drawn inward and turned from the man who wants to know everything without knowing himself to him who wants to know nothing, only to know himself. When later on Søren Kierkegaard not only turned away from the Greeks, but also turned against them, it was due to that barbaric feeling which was the natural bedrock of his genius, his fear, his melancholy. It prevented a profound assimilation of that humanistic balance which he has described in Assessor Vilhelm's figure and had known in Poul Møller, that inner harmony which distinguished the Greeks, including Socrates, though historically, as we know, the latter inaugurated the dissolution and individualisation and drove him from the teacher of humanism to the God who can save.—Kierkegaard's barbaric mind did not, however, manifest itself the first time, when he terminated the Greek line in his production in order to enter upon the Christian, when the Socratic Johannes Climacus was superseded by the paradoxical-Christian Anti-Climacus, it also determined the structure of the thought-building which he erected under Greek influence. With great brilliance Vilh. Andersen explains this in the second chapter of the section on Kierkegaard where, by a comparison of the exclamation which his fiancée's marriage evoked from the young man of "The Repetition" with Diotima's speech to Socrates in Plato's Symposium, he determines the nature of Kierkegaard's Hellenism. "It is not, like that of the preceding generation, Homeric, but Platonic. What Goethe praises Homer for, a limitation enamoured of reality, Plato calls petty and a sign of a slavish spirit. It was impossible for Kierkegaard to fall in love with anything individual, since like Plato he loved the Idea" (p. 71). This likeness between Plato and Kierkegaard can be read out of the two texts which both describe the transformation of the natural love impulse into a passion for thought; a comparison of the two authors' description of this metamorphosis will, on the other hand, inform us of their essential typological differences. "With Plato this metamorphosis takes place without any rupture by an evolution leading from "the æsthetic" (the beautiful bodies) through "the ethical" (the human occupations and customs) to the religious (the ideas). The childishly wise human thought builds its heaven-scaling ladder through all the zones of existence. Plato's view of life was, as Martensen would say, concentric, Kierkegaard's was eccentric. With him the life of the ideas sets in by a breach with the immediate existence, as a new element. To live in the idea is a perilous isolation, as in a dinghy on the great ocean. While the intellectual Eros is to the Greek who loved man like a love between two, the teacher and the pupil, the melancholy dweller in the North is alone in his highest aspiration, thrown back upon himself, torn out not only from the love that first kindled the idea in him, but deprived of every possible confidant." (p. 72). The discord in Søren Kierkegaard was present from the very first; he transferred it from his inner man to Christianity, which to him was a demand for the denial of the humane, the body as well as the mind.

A so-called immanent critical analysis will not afford any information of the scientific method adopted by Vilh. Andersen, for though his account of "the continued life of the thought of the ancients" in Kierkegaard's mind indeed shows exceptional erudition, it displays more art than real method. His use of quotations illustrates this fact. While the scientifically minded adduce Kierkegaardian notes to support their hypotheses with proofs and thus conclude with the quotation, Vilh. Andersen in his account starts from the quotation which with him serves the æsthetic mission of preparing and shedding light on his thought rather than proving its agreement with the truth. The quotation is the pass through which he lets his views go when they are to be transferred from his own to the reader's mind. But the Kierkegaard section in "Goethe" is not to be understood from the inside, but as part of the whole in which it appears. Søren Kierkegaard is not described as an individual but as a type, he is understood less through himself than through his contrast to J. L. Heiberg. The two represent the philosophy of continuity and discontinuity in the Platonic period of the 19th century, which adjoins respectively the Homeric (Oehlenschlæger—Thorvaldsen) and the Alexandrine (Brandes—Lange) periods. A criticism of Vilh. Andersen's exposition of Kierkegaard's relation to the tradition of antiquity must therefore be concerned with his culture-historical method; but to subject it to a closer investigation here would lead us too far from our subject. The chief peculiarity about Vilh. Andersen's "Ages and Types" is the very stringent, almost forced disposition revealing the author's highly developed sense of the pedagogical. The decisive question with regard to the chapters on Kierkegaard must then be whether he really can fill the place in the scheme assigned to him by Vilh. Andersen, or whether it has been necessary to strain a point to make him the philosopher of discontinuity among the Platonists of the 1840s. This does not seem to have been the case; Søren Kierkegaard may without constraint be brought to fill his place; what is said is right, but it is also merely a description.

The same subject, Kierkegaard's relation to Socrates has been treated by JENS HIMMELSTRUP (b. 1890; Phil. D. and D. L.) in his thesis for the doctorate (1924), but from a narrower angle; "Søren Kierkegaards Opfattelse af Sokrates "(S. K.'s Conception of Socrates), is its title, and the author expressly points out that an account of Socrates' significance for Kierkegaard's thinking and literary method thus does not come within the scope of his work (pp. 217-19). Owing to this Hermann Diem has put forward some objections; he thinks that Himmelstrup has drawn the limits for his field of work so as to confine himself to something comparatively indifferent, Kierkegaard's historical judgments, while the more important factor, Kierkegaard's discipleship-relation to Socrates, particularly with regard to the indirect communication, is left out of account. It is psychologically understandable why Diem of all men should raise this objection but it cannot for that reason be deemed unwarranted. It is undeniable that Himmelstrup has delimited his field of work in such a way that he must break off his investigations when they are just approaching the central Kierkegaardian problems; but as an introduction to a closer study of the relation between Socrates and Kierkegaard, the treatise cannot, owing to its point of view, be denied value.

According to Himmelstrup, Kierkegaard's interest in Socrates can be traced back to his earliest ponderings on the Romantic form of mentality. He has observed how the Romanticists, whose infinite aspirations the "world irony" has shattered, may develop a personal irony manifesting itself in the individual hovering above the world in "ironical satisfaction". And as early as the spring of 1837 he became aware that this latter form of irony was the Greek form which was especially represented by Socrates, who emancipated himself from the time and the society to which he belonged. Søren Kierkegaard's opinion of Socrates, however, did not remain unchanged from he discovered him in 1837 until he discusses him for the last time in "The Moment" in 1855. It is the nature and cause of the changes which Socrates' figure underwent in Kierkegaard's mind that Himmelstrup attempts to make clear in his thesis.—The fullest explanation of his view of Socrates Kierkegaard has given in his thesis for the M. A. degree: Socrates is there represented as the absolute negativity turning critically against the existing order of society, morals, and religion—as the negativity equipped with divine authority sweeping away all that is old in order that the new may break through. But he himself brings nothing new. He extracts from his disciples all that they possess of actual knowledge and imparts nothing positive to them instead. He is a judge, not a saviour. "And all this by virtue of irony. Irony is his form of expression. He is ironical in his intercourse with men, sometimes partially, sometimes totally, and irony at last carries Socrates with it,—carries him into the abyss. But irony is his point of view too. It is to him the principle in virtue of which he is absolutely negative, free, and in unfettered grace moves over the face of the waters—the principle of the non-existence of existence" (p. 60). The angle from which Søren Kierkegaard presents and appraises Socrates in the thesis is, Himmelstrup contends, the Hegelian. At the time of the thesis Kierkegaard was not precisely a Hegelian in the widest sense of the word, i.e. an adherent of the system, but he adhered absolutely to Hegel's historical and moral philosophical views. Hence he denies real virtues to Socrates and calls him downright immoral, because he has "emancipated himself from the true civic relation to the state"— and only he can be moral who bears a positive relation to the totality, and like Hegel and under the influence of Hegel he condemns the Romanticists and the untimely Romantic irony.—In the later production, especially in "Unscientific Postscript", we find another picture of Socrates. He is now the prototype of "the existing thinker", and his ignorance is regarded as expressing his realisation that subjectivity, intensity, is the truth; his ironical art of questioning is considered to be inspired by a love of the learner. Instead of the cold idealism, the negative infinity, which Kierkegaard saw embodied in Socrates' figure in his thesis, he now found a warm infinitude of humanity in him, and thus not only Kierkegaard's subjective evaluation but also his objective understanding of Socrates had changed in the period from 1840 to 1846. According to Himmelstrup, this change in Kierkegaard's view of Socrates is due primarily to the fact that in the period indicated (more precisely determined: in the course of the early summer and the autumn of 1841) he changed his ethical standpoint, rejecting the Hegelian ethics in favour of a pronounced individualistic ethic observable already in the second part of "Either—Or". Through this change Socrates comes to be seen by him in a sympathetic light, and thus Kierkegaard becomes aware of a so far unheeded element in his personality: his intensity. Behind the two different views of Socrates there are then two different ethical views; if the Socrates question is to be answered in a satisfactory way it must therefore be investigated why Kierkegaard at the close of the 30s and in the first year of the 40s shared Hegel's moral philosophical views, and why in the year 1841 he suddenly discarded them. —Himmelstrup finds the answer to these questions by an examination of Kierkegaard's personal life in the period 1835—41, an examination based on the above-discussed psychological literature, particularly P. A. Heiberg's "Segment". That Søren Kierkegaard's thesis shows such a strong Hegelian influence is due to the fact that it "stands as a part of the whole of that tendency shown by his aspirations from 1838. Wishing to get out of his intellectual isolation, of his feeling of being outside, and gradually trying to rise from the quagmire he feels he has got into, he looks about him for theoretical help, and in so far finds excellent support in Hegel. Here was exactly what he tremulously sought: firmness and security in the positive standpoint and, negatively, the sharp condemnation of that to which he had felt drawn, but which had only brought him sorrow and disappointment" (p. 172). And when Kierkegaard in "Either—Or" appears as a representative of an individualistic ethic, the transition to this new standpoint can be psychologically explained by the intellectual awakening that he experienced through his rupture with Regine, which led him socially into a state of isolation, philosophically into a number of meditations on the importance of the individual to the family, ending in a suggestion of the category of the abrupt leap. "The theoretical background for the category of "the single individual" is thus present. Ethically "the single individual" is characterised by a sharp negation of every ethic of totality; psychologically intensity is the decisive thing.—These were exactly the features we found in the Socrates of the production" (p. 215).

With this we have given an account of the main part of Himmelstrup's treatise, the central and disputed part. Two historical chapters on Kierkegaard as a figure in the study of Socrates, and one in which Kierkegaard's view of Socrates and his conception of Christ are compared, are left unmentioned. In spite of its inciting title the last chapter contains very little; it turns out that in his whole production Kierkegaard has unalterably regarded Socrates as the true witness to the truth, the highest man can attain, and Christ as the truth, man's saviour.

Himmelstrup's work has not met with much recognition among Kierkegaard researchers, especially the German ones. Schottländer, Diem, and Hirsch have raised almost uniform objections against Himmelstrup's contention that Kierkegaard's view of Socrates should have changed so essentially in the year 1841 that we can speak about two stages, and they have definitely denied that Kierkegaard, at the time of the thesis, was at the standpoint of the Hegelian ethic. Hirsch writes: "Himmelstrup has not seen the melancholy reserved depth of Kierkegaard's understanding of irony at that time and thus, because Kierkegaard is now more than later influenced by Hegel in the historical details of his conception of Socrates, he has mistaken the real intention of the work to turn Socrates against Hegel and so to find for the individual in his faith in God a contribution against speculation. From this evalution of the irony of Socrates to the indirect communication of the "Postscript" there is an unbroken line. I cannot therefore— — —find a change but only a deepening of the view of Socrates" (Studien II, p. 744). These critical remarks point in two directions: they give Hirsch's view of how Himmelstrup's conception deviates from what must be supposed to be the truth, and what may be the cause of this deviation. The two points will here be treated separately.

Hirsch thinks that the essential similarity between Hegel's and Kierkegaard's view of Socrates consists in dissimilarity. Hegel regards Socrates' irony as something external, a special form employed by him in his intercourse with others, and sees his importance in universal history in his introduction of new positive ideas concerning the true and the good. "With this exposition Kierkegaard is doubly at variance. Once he simply denies the positive in Socrates, hence conceives him as a negative phenomenon and regards irony as a suitable term for this phenomenon. Further, he sees the concept of irony in a deeper connection than Hegel. He thinks that beyond the Romantic attempt to make the concept absolute it has a meaning in human life, and he finds that Hegel has quite mistaken this meaning. Thus historically and fundamentally he becomes opposed to Hegel. This opposition is carried through consistently on the basis of his own reflective elaboration of the whole of the historical material of importance for Socrates as well as the whole of the Romantic fiction and view of the world. In details we may indeed often in this trace a dependence on Hegel's choice of material and presentation of problems, so much so that without a simultaneous reading of Hegel's account of Socrates and his remarks on irony an entirely wrong picture must emerge of Kierkegaard's intellectual independence; even his best independent observations have often a slight association with Hegel. He himself points out that Hegel often has individual observations of great force, standing isolated in the whole, and to be reconciled with it with difficulty. All this cannot, however, obscure the independence of the picture drawn of Socrates or the depth of the general conception turned against Hegel" (Studien II, pp. 592-93). If we compare the two quotations from Hirsch we might believe that Himmelstrup had not noticed at all the actual disagreement between Kierkegaard and Hegel; that is not the case, on the contrary he quite agrees with Hirsch in that respect: "As to the meaning of the two views Kierkegaard tries on two points to motivate an opinion deviating from that of Hegel: (1) it is an illusion when Hegel tries to ascribe to Socrates a certain positiveness, (2) Socrates' standpoint is irony.—To point out these two factors is as regards Hegel the real purpose of Kierkegaard's whole work" (p. 299). But their agreement goes no farther. In spite of his realisation of what is Kierkegaard's actual critical purpose in his relation to Hegel, Himmelstrup mostly regards his objections to Hegel's picture of Socrates as sophistic. "In the two differences mentioned there is a good deal that is only apparent—which can almost be reduced to a difference in the definition of terms, i.e. actually a dispute about words. If this were wholly the case Kierkegaard's view would objectively be the same as Hegel's. But this is not the case; there is a difference. Kierkegaard does really modify" (his view) (pp. 299-300). A little further on in the book the difference between Hegel's and Søren Kierkegaard's views is then given without further comment.—However, Hirsch and his predecessors in the criticism of Himmelstrup maintain that Kierkegaard's objections to Hegel have a perspective. He does not advance them in order to achieve merit as a philologist or a historian, but in the interests of true belief. When Kierkegaard polemises against Hegel because of his attempt to find something deeper in Socrates than irony, and maintains that Socrates was the infinite absolute negativity, and yet at the same time admits the truth of Hegel's observation that Socrates caused a change in the history of the world, it is according to Hirsch for the deliberate purpose of bringing Socrates, and so the humanities, back to religion. It was not because Socrates harboured positive virtues in his ironic figure, but because he acted as the instrument of the deity that his activity had such great consequences. (On this theory see further Hirsch, Studien II, pp. 591-602). That this interpretation of the view of Socrates presented in Kierkegaard's thesis is right, and that Himmelstrup's account is therefore misleading on an essential point can hardly be doubted. In this place it must suffice to quote one of the passages in Kierkegaard from which Hirsch draws support, and which indeed unambiguously points in the direction of his interpretation of the thesis. "In so far now as Socrates constantly let the self-existing appear, it might seem that in this at least he was in earnest; but just because he merely came to it, merely had the self-existing as the infinitely abstract, he had the absolute in the form of nothing. Reality in face of the absolute became nothing, but the absolute was again nothing. But in order to be able to keep him at this point, never to forget that the content of his life was that of making this movement in every element we must remember his importance as a divine messenger. This divine mission of his, Hegel has not heeded, even though Socrates lays such stress on it" (12, 336-37).

In Himmelstrup's treatise and in the discussion following the publication at the time it was established that Kierkegaard found his way to the Greeks with Hegel as his companion. Of the degree of his dependence no agreement was reached. The question could be taken up for a more all-round treatment in a treatise on Kierkegaard's debt to Hegel; but enquirers into Kierkegaard's thought have in a marked degree fought shy of the central problems, and treated the more peripherical ones as if the former had already been solved. Thus there exists no thorough account of Søren Kierkegaard's meaning with and practising of "indirect communication", nor of his relation to Hegel. Of the latter subject, apart from popular surveys there only exists one small study written by VICTOR KUHR (1882-1948), Professor of Philosophy in the University of Copenhagen from 1918 and co-editor of Kierkegaard's papers. Within the philosophical field his small book is what Heiberg's large books were within the biographical sphere, a demonstration of how the new edition of the Papers should be used according to the editors' opinion.

Kuhr mastered two styles, a popular one in which the difficult things were explained as if they were easy, this made him a popular teacher and lecturer, and an academical in which even the easiest things became difficult. It was the latter which he used with mastery in the small piece of logical microscopy which was to be his only independent contribution to Kierkegaard research: "Modsigelsens Grundsætning" (The Principle of Contradiction; Kierkegaard Studier II, 1915).

On the first page of the treatise the disapsalma beginning, "Tautology is and remains the highest principle, the highest maxim of thinking" (I, 25), is compared with a note connected with "Either—Or" (III B 177), in which tautology is asserted to be the scientific expression of the principle of contradiction. Then the following question is raised: (1) "Would it be possible to connect this consideration with other developments of thought in "A's Papers"; (2) and would it be feasible historically to follow its—probably polemically determined—genesis, (3) and perhaps its relation to the further development of Kierkegaard's thought?"

It should be possible, though it would not be possible to retain the clear disposition of the question. The ingenious analysis cannot here be followed in detail but it should be mentioned that the results, inter alia, are procured by a careful commentary on Søren Kierkegaard's expressions which excellently illustrates how dangerous it is to give witty interpretations of Kierkegaard's unexpected formulations. Thus e.g. the examination of the concept "infinite judgments" used in the above-mentioned disapsalma in a connection excluding the habitual Aristotelian definition, leads back to a category of infinite judgments erected by Hegel, which stands quite isolated in the history of logic.—The result of the treatise, distributed in answers to the three questions, is: (1) That fundamentally the æsthete A keeps to the principle of contradiction; but owing to his purely intellectual relation to existence he can construct opposed possibilities out of every phenomenon of reality, or conversely declare that the realisation of opposed possibilities gives the same result (marry or do not marry, you will regret both); this use of the principle of contradiction may be called tautological, since to the æsthete the opposites in reality coincide because they are equally valid to him in relation to existence; either—or under the aspect of tautology becomes neither-nor. In this way not only "An ecstatic Lecture" from the Diapsalmata, but also the "The Rotation Method" and several smaller apostrophes in A's notes are brought under the principle of tautology. (2) That Kierkegaard, already in 1839, privately took Mynster's part in a literary dispute on the principle of contradiction, in which Mynster in opposition to the Copenhagen Hegelians Heiberg and Martensen asserted the absolute validity of the principle of contradiction and exclusion. (3) Hence to the æsthete who is "prior to reality" the principle of contradiction becomes a jest, tautology. The principle of contradiction, however, also entered into Kierkegaard's continued thinking and is implied in his erection of the religious category "the paradox", the irrational unity of absolute opposites to which the person who would harbour more than reality in his mind must cling.

In the treatise by the theologian Julius Schousboe (b. 1886) "Om Begrebet Humor hos Søren Kierkegaard" (On the Concept of Humour in Søren Kierkegaard; 1925)—a most peculiar work regarded as a thesis for the doctorate—a movement from the humane to the Christian is described, which runs parallel to the line from Socrates to Christ drawn by Vilh. Andersen in his depiction of Kierkegaard. But while this line arises naturally in Vilh. Andersen's book because Kierkegaard's spiritual development is viewed against the background of the general cultural history, with Schousboe it is the result of a strange procedure which, briefly described, consists in considering Søren Kierkegaard and the concept of humour each against the background of the other. This peculiar fact is explained by the history of the origin of Schousboe's work, which shall therefore be given here in abbreviated form. Since his freshman year Schousboe had occupied himself with the central religious problem of the relation between faith and experience and noted the authors who expressed thoughts related to his own. "Then Gerhard Gran's book on religious unrest appeared. In these views I seemed to feel the pulse of the time, nay, not only that of a single period of time, but that of mankind; through these thoughts I felt that I was led into one of the eternal truths of man: the religious craving and right of the personality to believe. With renewed eagerness I tried to collect these thoughts under the aspect: the conflict of the personality with the problem of knowledge, but where was one to begin or conclude when faced by one of man's eternal truths which in various conflicts appeared in varying garb but always with the same meaning.—I had to seek a definite limit, a definite field, in order to make these thoughts come out clearly. For a time I thought that it could best be found in Pascal, then I thought of taking my starting point in a comparison between William James's and Kierkegaard's thoughts on the subject. I had already long understood that Kierkegaard's humorous stage would come prominently into consideration. And finally I sought my circumscribed starting-point there" (Preface p. VIII). From these lines it will appear that Schousboe's treatise has a double source, being the fruit partly of ponderings on the religious problem, partly of studies of Kierkegaard's writings. The consequence has been, what it need not have been, that the treatise can now neither be said to come under Kierkegaard research nor under philosophy. For Schousboe has not given priority to one of the starting points, and thus chosen either to examine Kierkegaard's conception of the concept of humour and given up a more abstract treatment of the antithetic relation: religion—experience, or to make this subject the central point in his treatise and then discussed Kierkegaard's humorous stage in one of the sections. But he has allowed the two points of view to conflict with each other, on the one hand letting his interest in Søren Kierkegaard confine his occupation with the problem of faith to an examination of the concept of humour, and on the other hand being too personally engrossed in the religious question to confine himself to a literary analysis of Kierkegaard's changing conception of the meaning of the term and therefore viewing the whole of Søren Kierkegaard, i.e. his person, his form of communication, and his writings against the background of the concept of humour. The double interest which inspired Schousboe's work therefore recurs in his thesis as a dual point of view determining the structure of the whole as well as the individual sections.

The first chapter gives the definitions of humour of a large number of philosophers and æsthetes; it turns out that despite considerable differences in the precise determination of the term it is generally agreed that there is "an element which must be designated as a fundamental characteristic of humour, and that is its combination of the comic and the tragic" (p. 16). In what follows the various forms of humour are described, first in their quantitative mounting from humour as a form of communication, via humour as an element in disposition and character, to humour as a view of life, then in their qualitative difference within the individual forms, and finally in their quantitative decrease from humour as a view of life, via humour as a limit to religion, to humour as an incognito to religion.—Already from this it will be seen that Schousboe's classification is partly achieved by speculation, partly by an investigation of Kierkegaard's practical and theoretical relation to "the unity of the tragic and the comic". In the disposition of the main section of the treatise this dualism does not assert itself so vigorously because here the exposition centres round those kinds of humour which Kierkegaard has treated theoretically; it is the Christian kind, represented by Hamann who takes an absolutely sceptic view of finiteness, but reconciles himself to it by regarding it from the secure station of eternity; the demoniacal kind practised especially by Heine, which is at the same time bound to the temporal and despises it, and therefore expresses itself in the bitter despairing laughter; and finally the sad sympathetic humour embodied by Kierkegaard in the figure of Johannes Climacus. In it the antitheses of life, the tragic and the comic, are reconciled in one fundamental mood which finds its expression in a resigned smile, in sad and sceptic sympathy with life. It is this feeling of totality towards life that Høffding has called "the great humour" and explained as a psychic state originating in a belief in the persistence of value. But Høffding differs from Kierkegaard by the fact that he regards the stage of humour as the highest, which Kierkegaard cannot do because the absolutely tragic seems to him to be the final reality of the purely human existence. "In Kierkegaard's opinion, the humorous must always be wrecked on the tragic since he asserts that any view of life which is outside a religious understanding of life is in itself absolutely tragic, or as Anti-Climacus has it, that there has not lived and does not live any man outside Christianity without being in despair and in Christendom none, in so far as he is not a true Christian, and that the opposite of despairing is to believe" (p. 269). To Søren Kierkegaard therefore the humorous stage becomes the limit of the religious stage, the last humane stage from which man in despair is driven to religion and to the belief of a transcendental solution to the problems of life.

Not a few objections might be raised against Schousboe's work, both from a general philosophical point of view against his treatment of the concept of humour, which in his interpretation has the same peculiarities as "the word Schnur in the dictionary", and from a Kierkegaardian point of view against his demonstration of a continuous movement from the human to the religious, but what has already been said above about the internal lack of harmony caused by the dual point of view must here suffice also as an explanation of the fact that Schousboe's book only occupies a very modest and obscure place within modern Kierkegaard research.

B. *Søren Kierkegaard and the Theological Tradition*

In the introduction to this treatise it was shown that Kierkegaard's work had been studied from three different points of view, the first of which, implying an absolute acceptance of Søren Kierkegaard's assertion of having used indirect communication, being only represented among German enquirers. In the theological part of Scandinavian Kierkegaard research the conflict between the two other viewpoints, the totality- and the part-view, has evoked tension and a prolonged polemic between the two Swedish theologians, Bishop TORSTEN BOHLIN (1889-1950) and Professor of theology in the University of Åbo VALTER LINDSTRÖM (b. 1907) who has made the chief contribution within the sphere. The polemics ended as polemics always end: none of the problems were elucidated, and none of the parties was convinced that his opponent was right.

Torsten Bohlin builds up his studies from isolated analyses of Kierkegaard's various writings and in this way claims to have demonstrated the presence of a marked lack of agreement in his production manifested partly as an inner synchronic contrast in Kierkegaard's dogmatic views, partly as a diachronic contrast in his ethical views. Polemising against this procedure and its results Lindström holds that the question of Kierkegaard's theological and moral views cannot be treated as isolated problems at all or be answered by analyses of his various writings, but that his remarks concerning humane and religious subjects must be seen against the background of his general view. If this method is adopted it will appear that apparently contradictory utterances of Kierkegaard's enter into one great common denominator. In the introduction to his treatise on the theology of the Stages Lindström says: "The main principle of this investigation must be to try to understand Kierkegaard's world of thought as a unitary view. In the case of apparent contradictions the question must always be put whether a defining of the meaning of the concepts in the judgments which apparently are at variance with each other may not solve the difficulties. In the case of a man of Kierkegaard's standard we must quite simply take it for granted that seemingly opposed tendencies are in some way held together by a general view. Above all this must be the case with a thinker so thoroughly reflective as Kierkegaard to whom continuity in life and thought and the mutual agreement of these quantities are of decisive importance. A unitary total view must therefore be assumed which forms the background of, and is reflected in, the edifying writings as well as the "æsthetic" production" (pp. 10-11).

The results of Bohlin's and Lindström's works will be presented in the sequel. No final criticism where the author tries to judge or mediate between the two theologians will be given. The conflicting views must remain unreconciled. For in these works viewpoints and methods are so closely connected that an isolated criticism of the method would be meaningless. And as was pointed out in the introduction, both points of view seem unsatisfactory.—Bohlin's books will here be reviewed in inverse chronological order because his exposition of the changes in Kierkegaard's ethical views implies a knowledge of his account of the inner discord in Kierkegaard's dogmatic thinking.

It is right, Bohlin admits in the introductory chapter of his voluminous book "Kierkegaards dogmatiska åskådning" (Kierkegaard's dogmatic View, 1925), that in his teaching of Christianity Kierkegaard strongly emphasised that from a religious point of view the decisive thing is a how and not a what; but he never went so far in his subjectivity as to declare the content of the faith to be of no consequence, on the contrary, he subjected the dogmatic problems bearing a relation to the faith of the individual, i.e. sin and faith, to extensive investigations in which he assumed an independent attitude towards orthodoxy.—According to Bohlin, Søren Kierkegaard, without knowing it, advocated two opposed conceptions of sin, which can both be observed in all his writings where the subject of sin is treated. But the fact is that one conception of sin is dominant in "The Concept of Dread" and "The Sickness unto Death", the other in "Philosophical Fragments" and "Unscientific Postscript". In this treatise, where our object is not to give Bohlin's analyses but their results, the clash of the two conceptions of sin in the individual works will not be discussed, but will each of them be identified without qualification with the publications in which they are predominant.—In the two psychological works sin is voluntaristically determined; it is characterised partly as an enigmatic force, at once alluring and alarming, which, when it has seized upon man's will, throws him into despair and makes him powerless, so that only faith will give him strength to rise to a new life, partly as a phenomenon belonging to the world of freedom, to which man therefore cannot enter into any relation without incurring personal guilt. That Kierkegaard, in his books on dread and despair, can at the same time recognise moral liberty as a reality and sin as an unconquerable force, is due to the fact that he wrote these books from his personal religious experience of the reality of sin and freedom, of the unapproachable inaccessible "something", that tremendous and fascinating mystery called by the religious philosopher Otto the numinous, and denoting the irrational element in the deity. In the "Fragments" and the "Postscript" the concept of sin is intellectualistically determined; sin is not here regarded as the expression of a decision of the will in conscious conflict with the recognised truth, but as a paradoxical transformation of the human reason which occurs at the birth of man and is thus one with his nature. From this form of sin, therefore, not only can one never be saved by oneself, but even by God only by a miracle of creation, by which the condition for understanding the truth is imparted to the existing person who is thereby radically changed. This concept of sin is not derived from personal religious experiences, but on the contrary, is so greatly at variance with the basic Christian experience that man, by acquiring faith, loses his continuity with his natural ego, that from a Christian point of view it must be regarded as false and remote from reality. If nevertheless it is claimed by Kierkegaard to be a specifically Christian conception of sin, it is because the doctrine of Christianity taught in the "Fragments" and the "Postscript" is determined by the desire to let the belief in Christ as the absolute paradox mould every point of the Christian view of life. Hence it turns out that Kierkegaard has given two fundamentally different definitions of the concept of sin, one lying in the line of religious experience, the other in the line of the paradox in his dogmatic thinking. —The question of faith is answered in the same double way as the question of sin. In "The Concept of Dread" and in "The Sickness unto Death" faith is represented simply as the opposite of sin, i.e. as community of will with God. And even though Kierkegaard did not himself take up the subject of dread—faith for treatment, yet it appears with all plainness from his psychological writings that faith is related in nature to the elements in dread which can be called the human-numinous or the unfathomable "something" by which the consciousness of God is immanent in man. In the "Fragments" and the "Postscript", on the other hand, faith is identified with the belief that Christ was at the same time God and man; the mere theoretical recognition of the doctrine of the dual nature is not there regarded as sufficient to constitute faith, but yet as strictly necessary. In these writings therefore the concept of faith is deduced from the idea of Christianity as a contrast to speculation, as the absolute paradox. "Thus the analysis of the fundamental determinations of faith in Kierkegaard ends in the result that it is two altogether different conceptions of faith that clash, one of which is theoretically determined while the other is in a special sense christocentrically determined, and the former of which belongs to the personally religious line of experience, while the other goes back to a marked view of the special nature of Christianity as opposed to other theological trends" (pp. 254-55).—However, the fact is that the dualism in Kierkegaard's dogmatic thought that was indicated above is only roughly expressed in the contrast between his image of God and his image of Christ. In reality there is an interaction, the numinous relation to God being incorporated in his determination of the figure of Christ, while the paradox-idea has penetrated into his image of God. This appears upon an examination of his various explanations of the Christian faith. Kierkegaard considers man's situation dialectical; on the one hand man must incessantly endeavour to resemble Christ, on the other hand the prototype crushes man's efforts by its absoluteness, but at the moment when the existing person has reached despair at his wickedness it is transformed into everlasting mercy. This duality has been expressed by Kierkegaard in the word contemporaneity, which partly contains the demand that the individual must make himself contemporaneous with the abased Christ and undertake the heavy duty of imitation, partly the glad tidings of the exalted Christ who is eternally present and forgives man for his sins. Thus the Christian faith acquires the character of being at the same time activity and receptivity, being based on Christ both as a prototype and a redeemer, as a demand and as a gift. Forgiveness is that gift of God which the believer shall receive day by day again and again and which shall deliver him from the old life under the power of sin and lead him into a new life; but of these two consequences of forgiveness Kierkegaard only seems to have described and personally experienced the former. However strongly he may emphasise that Christ brings joy and good cheer, he does chiefly regard forgiveness from the point of view that God pours his infinite riches into the believer's heart after the obstacle to full communion has been removed. To Kierkegaard the assurance of faith does not mean the possession of, but the hope of, salvation; this disagreement is due to the fact that in his fundamental determination of the new life of forgiveness there enters a metaphysical element owing to which the community of will with God which was to follow upon forgiveness cannot be realised but is only an ideal. In his concept of God ethical religious views are combined with abstract-metaphysical. God is defined partly as sovereign and holy love, partly as a being absolutely different from man in quality, and when Kierkegaard speaks of the transformation of man in God's image as a consequence of forgiveness he is thinking of this eternal and absolute being. The task to be solved by the believer therefore will not be the overcoming of sin and the hallowing of the will, but death to immediacy, the radical breach with natural human life.

The previous explanation (cf. p. 54 f.) of how this heterogeneous element has gained access to Kierkegaard's religion is, according to Bohlin, not sufficient. That the intellectual-metaphysical view has come to pervade Kierkegaard's whole teaching of Christianity is not primarily due to his dependence on the Athanasian doctrine of the dual nature, but on his double relation to the Hegelian religious philosophy. To Hegel Christianity meant the reconciliation of the finite and the infinite; he regarded the figure of Christ as a manifestation of the essential identity of the divine and the human. This speculative interpretation of Christianity was regarded by Kierkegaard as an extreme danger to the true faith, and he tried to destroy it by energetically asserting the absolute qualitative difference between God and man. He conceded to Hegel that Christ in himself combined the infinite and the finite, but denied that this fact could be accepted as an expression of a theoretical reconciliation. On the contrary, he declared that the unity of the eternal and the temporal in Christ is the paradoxical fact to which faith is unconditionally bound and which constitutes its fundamental difference from speculative thinking. In order to secure more favourable conditions for aiming a death blow at Hegel's conclusion concerning the nature of Christianity Kierkegaard, however, took over Hegel's premises. His polemics against Hegel's attempt to adopt a metaphysical view of Christianity actually rest on the Hegelian categories and metaphysical distinctions (finite-infinite, temporal-eternal, nature-spirit). "But this involves that, however emphatically Kierkegaard has asserted the irrational character of Christianity against the intellectualism of Hegel's conception of religion, irrationalism with him includes a marked intellectualistic element. And this is the reason why Kierkegaard also, despite the strong emphasising of the historical revelation, has not been able to avoid spiritualising the latter, not indeed like Hegel to a general Christ-principle, but to a paradox in which man knows himself to be absolutely separate from God" (pp. 435-36).—The intellectualism that gained access to Kierkegaard's mind in the contest against Hegel came to exert an inhibiting influence on the primary constitutive element of his faith, the personal religious experience, and therefore hindered his entire acceptance of Luther's doctrine of Christianity. The spiritual freedom and richness contained in Luther's conception of faith and mercy Søren Kierkegaard could not personally acquire because by establishing the absolute qualitative difference between God and man he had made the new life of faith a practical impossibility.

The idea of God as a being absolutely different in quality from man which, according to Bohlin, has been of decisive importance for Kierkegaard's attitude to the dogmatic problems and is a consequence of an intellectualistic train of thought heterogeneous from the religious, has, in the same author's opinion, also exerted considerable influence on Kierkegaard in another respect; the abstract-metaphysical concept of God entered as a ferment into his ethical views and caused their slow but radical transformation, the results of which are presented in "Søren Kierkegaards etiska åskådning" (Søren Kierkegaard's ethical View; 1918). This book which is seven years older than the above-mentioned, will here be reviewed with special reference to its account of the currents in Kierkegaard's ethics. Hence the introductory, not very important, chapters on the historical antecedents of Kierkegaard's production and its special peculiarities will be passed over; in this way we shall avoid unnecessary repetitions.

The first full presentation of his ethical views is given by Kierkegaard in the treatises in the second part of "Either—Or". These indeed are written by Assessor Vilhelm, who must not of course be identified with Kierkegaard, but on close inspection the two, the pseudonym and the real author, prove to be kindred spirits. Assessor Vilhelm represents an ethic, the special peculiarity of which consists in equal consideration for the social and the individual. The dual trend is expressed in the ethical main category "the common lot" which demands of the individual that he shall try to become common man; this demand is not the positive formulation of an interdiction of the individualistic striving to become one's self in the deepest sense. On the contrary, this very striving to assert one's self is the right expression of the duty to realise the "common lot". For the true self is the concrete self equipped with certain individual qualities and placed in a particular environment, a particular community. The individual ethical task will then be to perform the duties imposed upon one as a citizen and member of the community. "The aim of his striving the individual has in himself, but this self he does not understand in the abstraction of isolation but only in full concreteness; to that concreteness belong the factors through which the individual stands in a relation of interaction to the world and the people around him. The self which is the aim of his striving is thus a social and civic self just as much as it is a purely personal self. As a concequence the common man whom the ethical man is to create will only be realised by the individual alternately living in the purely personal and the civic sphere. From the personal life he moves to the civic, from this again he moves back to the personal. Through this, the personality shall become more and more open to the rich content of reality, and this content gives to the personality its ever higher form" (pp. 159-60). The essential condition for the unlimited validity of the ethical demand for expressing the common lot in the individual must be that every man, if he so desires, can comply with it. But Assessor Vilhelm is aware that there are people who in spite of good will are not able fully to realise the common lot. To such an individual, he thinks, there is nothing to be done but to emancipate himself deliberately from the common lot in respect of the point impossible for him to overcome, and to accompany this behaviour by a recognition of the sublimity of the common lot, and regret at his own limitations. This admission of the justification of the exceptional man, however conditional, proves to be the manifestation of a tendency which gradually becomes more and more opposed to the ordinary human ethical trend. The exception ends by threatening the very existence of the ethical stage. The beginning of this movement away from the common lot may already be plainly observed in "Fear and Trembling". For what is there stated to be the obstacle to the realisation of the ethical ideal is not an individual limitation, but the relation to God. By a description of Abraham's behaviour to Isaac it is shown that the absolute obedience to God which is part of faith, may force a man to perform ethically objectionable actions and so necessitate a theological suspension of the ethical. Thus two facts emerge upon an investigation of "Fear and Trembling", namely that Søren Kierkegaard's ethical views are moving in an individualistic direction and that this movement is religiously determined.—The fundamental breach with the ethical stage only takes place, however, with the transition to the Christian production, i.e. with the "Philosophical Fragments" and "The Concept of Dread". For a new category is introduced, causing a general suspension of the ethical; this is sin, which like an all-embracing enigmatical reality is present in each single individual and makes every ethical striving impossible. "The suspension is here not determined by the absolute duty but it is determined by man's powerlessness, due to his own fault, to realise the ethical. And this standpoint which negates the ethical, in comparison with the standpoint of the ethical stage, implies a higher view altogether in the same sense as Christianity is higher than heathenism" (p. 215). The recognition of Christianity as the highest truth necessitates the erection of an entirely new ethic, which is not determined by the relation of the individual to the common lot, but by the relation of the individual to the paradox of faith. This Christian ethic was presented by Kierkegaard in the "Unscientific Postscript". The demand to be complied with is that of being "the single individual". In this category, which replaces the concept of the exceptional, is implied not only that each single man must personally decide upon his attitude to the religious problem but also that he must try to comply with the demands of faith, which according to Kierkegaard are that the individual must stand in an absolute relation to the absolute telos and in a relative relation to the relative. In principle a positive attitude towards the temporal is allowed, but actually this can never be realised, because the religious endeavour to establish a relation to the being of an absolutely different quality from man claims all the energy of the personality. "The single individual's" attitude to the finite therefore becomes purely negative; his inner state is characterised by suffering, which arises out of the endeavour to annihilate the earthly ego for God, his outer state by isolation because the ethically existing individual only knows and has a duty to a reality, his own self. The ethical views Kierkegaard holds in the "Unscientific Postscript" are not essentially altered in the production that follows from "A literary Review" to and including "The Moment". On the one hand, it is emphasised with increasing strength that suffering is the distinguishing feature of the believer's existence and the martyr is represented as the ethical ideal. On the other hand, the polemics against the common human lot, the civic life, are intensified and concluded in "The Moment" with a condemnation of marriage, the Church, and altogether everything bearing a positive relation to the temporal world. But actually this only means that Kierkegaard has drawn the ultimate conclusions from that conception of Christianity which was developed in the "Unscientific Postscript". The transition from Assessor Vilhelm's humane ethics in "Either—Or" to the rigidly ascetic and misanthropic ethics asserted in "The Moment" is thus due to Kierkegaard's faith, more precisely to his abstract-metaphysical concept of God and can be observed in his changing determinations of the category of the exception.

Valter Lindström's book "Stadiernas Teologi" (The Theology of the Stages, 1943) falls into two parts, the first of which comprises three chapters and corresponds to Bohlin's exposition of Kierkegaard's dogmatic views, while the second part consists of 6 chapters dealing with the same subject which Bohlin discusses in his studies on Kierkegaard's ethics. The circumstance that the younger author treats in one book the same subjects as the elder distributes over two, illustrates their disagreement in principle. For Lindström begins his book with three lengthy chapters on the structure of the relation to God from a conviction that the problem of the Stages cannot be solved at all, their individual works cannot be understood, unless they are viewed against the background of Kierkegaards' conception of the nature of faith, which conviction in its negative aspect means a ban on presenting Kierkegaard's ethical views without always taking into consideration his dogmatic opinions. If the account of Lindström's book that follows is compared with the preceding account of Bohlin's it will be plainly seen how different Søren Kierkegaard seems from the two opposed standpoints.

The foundation of Kierkegaard's thought is "the inescapability" (ofrånkomlighet) of the relation to God". This formula contains the postulate that every human being, believer or non-believer, has a relation to God. By the creation he is bound to Him and belongs so completely to Him in thought and feeling that He cannot be conceived as a phenomenon outside consciousness; God is the subject not the object of human thought. Man is created in God's image and, therefore, in contrast with all other creatures, has been endowed with an eternal self, an absolute spirit. This special position entails both duties and dangers; the fact that man has been given a spirit again obliges him to recognise God as the creator of himself and all things, and to obey his will, but on the other hand, gives him the possibility of denying and defying God. Man has taken advantage of this possibility, he has sinned and so erected the infinite qualitative difference between himself and God. "Man has then, in Kierkegaard's conception, been created as spirit to be God's image, i.e. as a free and responsible creature to do God's will. As a sinner, however, man defies this intention of God's. But since the designation of man as spirit and God's image does not to Kierkegaard imply the assumption of man's unity of nature with the divine, even though in both cases—conversely—the demand that man shall be like God is implied, Kierkegaard can talk of sinful man as spirit and God's image, even though he is radically different from God through his sin. That he is spirit testifies to the inescapability of the relation to God, and man's special position and precedence of other created beings may therefore, with the dualism in view, be said to consist in his possibility of despairing" (pp. 113-14).—The task Kierkegaard wanted to solve by his exposition of the stages of human life was to describe how the individual traverses the distance, which by his sin he has interposed between himself and God. The distance from the state of natural man, characterised by more or less disguised attempts to rid himself of God, to that of the true believer which can be described as community of will with the creator. The type of man farthest from God is the æsthete; his stage is that of the absence of spirituality, which does not mean that he is without spirit but that he is not conscious of himself as spirit, as everybody can and ought to be. The qualities of his personality for and on which the æsthete lives are the relatively significant: talent, gifts, beauty, and therefore, at variance with his eternal destiny, he becomes bound to temporality, and loses his footing and despairs, as soon as the world goes against him. He who lives æsthetically may thus be said to have his centre in the periphery; whereas the ethical personality has its centre in itself. One may rise to his standpoint from the æsthetic by choosing one's absolute self (i.e. the concrete and civic self) as the law of one's life. Thus the ethical person should not order his life according to common norms and principles, but should try to comply with the demands inherent in his self, in order to bring himself into accordance with God's will. In this way he enters into a relation to the paradox that the individual is higher than the common law, for he must read the law for his actions out of his inner man. "The eternal or the ethical is determined individually, with the consequence that each person can only conceive the ethical in himself. That is his "co-knowledge" with God. The ethical cannot be grasped by man except in a concrete situation and at a particular moment, and he cannot be possessed of the truth in any other way than through a decision by action; subjectivity is the truth. The counterpart to this thesis is the proposition that the truth objectively determined is a paradox" (p. 233). In the phase of existence succeeding the ethical, i.e. the ethical-religious or religiousness A, the demand is the same; nevertheless the situation is changed because here man stands in another relation to the infinite demand. Of the ethical person it is characteristic that in the performance of his duties he preserves the belief that he can comply with the demand by the aid of his own strength. But this confidence shows that he is still remote from the absolute relation to God. The boundlessness of this relation is understood by the ethical religious person, who at the same time understands that in his life he stands in an absolute relation to the relative and thus incurs guilt. He will then try to realise the true relation to God by striving towards "death to immediacy"; this does not mean to isolate himself from community with human beings. "The aim of resignation is therefore nothing but the Pauline aim, to use this world as if one did not use it. "He lives in the finite, but he has not his life in it". There is no question of the existing person becoming indifferent to worldly tasks. But the absolute respect is for the absolute telos, not for the finite" (pp. 279-280). This painful way to God, however, proves to be barred, as the ethical religious person will experience when he meets the revelation of God in Christ, confronted with whom man becomes conscious of his sins, as a being poisoned by original sin who is radically severed from the eternal truth. This knowledge necessitates a complete breach with the humane; by the consciousness of sin the existing person is forced into the Christian existential sphere, religiousness B, which is characterised by the belief in the absolute paradox, the God in time. This belief brings man the forgiveness of sins and thus the possibility of beginning a new life. "When he (man) in faith grasps the forgiveness of sins this involves a transition from death to life. God Himself in Christ takes up His abode in him, His spirit lives in him and causes a divine growth. He is made a limb of Christ's body and a co-operator of God. His salvation implies that God, in spite of man's sin which defies His creative will, still cares for him" (p. 329). Man is created anew and by God led back to that reality in which he is to live and act and which he nearly left in his efforts to die to the world. "The stirring of faith shall give reality back to man and prepare the way for him to enter into the texture of creation according to God's will" (p. 330). It is this movement from world to world through Christianity which Kierkegaard calls "repetition" or "the double movement of infinity".

These views of man's relation to God and the world which have been described above have been given expression by Kierkegaard in the first series of pseudonymous writings. It is, however, according to Lindström, the same general outlook which is behind his whole religious production; the great emphasis laid on the imitation in the later writings has probably involved "a gliding away from the fundamental attitude", but not a revision of the basic ideas.

In the polemics of Lindström and Bohlin following the publication of "The Theology of the Stages", Bohlin's book "Kierkegaard's Faith" (1944) is one of the most important documents. Here Bohlin amongst other things criticises Lindström because his treatise is based upon a too limited onesided selection of Kierkegaard's production so charged with tension; and he asserts that Lindström's account of the transition from the confirmatory outlook of the Stages to the ascetic and negative teaching of "The Moment" shows that actually he has observed the break in Kierkegaard's ethical development, though verbally he obscures it by designating it as a "gliding" without any fundamental consequences.—Opposed to these objections we have Lindström's assertion that Bohlin's results, according to which Kierkegaard without being aware of it himself advocated contradictory views, not only within the same phase of his production but in the same treatise, are psychologically improbable. And to this psychological improbability may be added the incontrovertible fact that Kierkegaard again and again emphasised that he was not professing opinions but trying to rouse people to a knowledge of themselves, that he raised problems but gave several equally valid solutions of them. Thus there is much to induce us, with Hirsch, to regard Repetition—Fear and Trembling as dual works like "Either—Or", and if we do so there is no reason to be surprised that the author of the authors may seem to disagree with himself. But none of these remarks settles the dispute between the two theologians. The fact is that those parts of Kierkegaard's production which one of them can explain and fit into his system, the other is obliged to leave alone.

It must be possible to find the higher unity into which these conflicting views can be merged, or at least a position relative to the production from which the growth-points for the opposite lines of interpretation can be surveyed. An æsthetic literary investigation of the production absolutely maintaining the distinction between the public writings and the private notes and trying to demonstrate the contrast between the isolated themes in the diaries and the circumscribed themes of the work, between the different meanings and style of the various pseudonyms, would perhaps be able to arrive at the clarity now lacking and point out where there were connections and breaks according to the new lines. Such an investigation has not been made, but it may at any rate be said that it need not be held back for want of material or encouragement on the part of Kierkegaard; his works and papers contain a wealth of suggestions concerning these subjects which so far have not been turned to account.

4. Conclusion. The General Biographies of the Period

The division of the work and the interrelation of the methods adopted in the second period of Kierkegaard research have been so fully treated during our survey of the works that there is nothing essential to add. The differentiation of the study is the dominant feature of the period and consequently there is no common denominator into which the various works can enter. No actual characterisation of the period can therefore be given.

Instead we shall conclude with a survey of the larger general expositions written in the period; from these an idea can be formed of how large a part of the results of the specialised studies has been generally accepted and enters into the popularly written and most widely read books.

Incomparably the most widely read work on Søren Kierkegaard is "Søren Kierkegaard's Development and Authorship" 1-6 (1926-28) by EDUARD GEISMAR (1871-1939). Geismar, who was a clergyman and from 1921 Professor of Systematic Theology in the University of Copenhagen, is by the Danish public and also abroad regarded as the greatest Danish authority on Søren Kierkegaard. The reason is probably that Geismar was the first to avail himself of the many specialised studies of the 20th century for a comprehensive and popular general exposition; as such his book is indeed undoubtedly valuable. It is thorough and entertaining, it is based on the whole Kierkegaard literature of the time and on life-long study of and absorption in Kierkegaard's writings. But Geismar lacks an independent opinion on the subject, not in his reply to the individual questions, but in the presentation of the problem, and he brings his work into a doubtful relation to actual research by his constant reference to personal religious experience; and by his highly confessional style.

Geismar's work falls into 6 parts, of which the first and fourth parts are in the main biographical, dealing with Kierkegaard's history and development 1813-41 (i.e. to and including the breaking off of the engagement to Regine); the second and fifth parts record, cite, and analyse the pseudonymous and edifying production respectively; the third part deals with Kierkegaard's philosophy in the reactionary dependence on Hegel, the sixth part with the onslaught on the Church. As previously mentioned, the books have been prepared on the basis of the whole Kierkegaard literature of the time, but the main sources are P. A. Heiberg's and to a smaller extent Bohlin's books. The relative value of Geismar's contribution was precisely that at so early a stage he made Heiberg's biographical and Bohlin's theological studies accessible in a coherent popular account. But Geismar did not do so without some reservation as regards a multiplicity of individual results, and so we feel in his books a peculiar mixing of temperaments; they have as it were two strata, a substratum of hard-handed method and unshakable systematics, and a surface where the views are constantly changing, the method fails, and private religious experiences form weighty links in the chain of argument.—In his explanation of the course of Kierkegaard's development in the critical years 1835-38 Geismar adheres absolutely to Heiberg's "Episode" and "Segment" in all main features, but goes his own special way when he comes to the results. Søren Kierkegaard's scandalised indignation with his father and with Christianity in the autumn of 1835 is explained by the circumstance that he learned about his father's so-called sexual offence; this event is described in poetic form in "Solomon's Dream". The "Earthquake" is assigned to 1838—on account of the marginal note: 25 years. The cause of it, Geismar thinks, is a secret which Kierkegaard took with him in his grave. "If any inquisitive person should wish to wrest this secret from him by letting his imagination run riot, then God is more merciful than such a man and after his death he has preserved his confidant's suffering from profanation" (I, p. 72). It is possible, but then any motive for making "Solomon's Dream" subserve the personal history falls away. Ever since Brandes in 1877 expressed his opinion that "Solomon's Dream" represented an event which had taken place between Kierkegaard and his father, the proof of the correctness of this assertion has been that the said insertion was a downright recasting of the "Earthquake". If the "Earthquake" and "Solomon's Dream" are separated, every right to read autobiography into Kierkegaard's description of the relation between David and his son falls away.

And indeed Geismar got into difficulties by using two such different minds as Heiberg and Bohlin as his sources. Heiberg is the only student of Kierkegaard who has regarded his life as a continued increase in his religious convictions, culminating in the onslaught on the Church. In contrast with him Bohlin has regarded a part of Kierkegaard's thoughts as religiously inspired, and another, that which came to dominate the later production, as intellectualistic, un-Lutheran, and un-Christian. Geismar mediates both methods and opinions and does so by prolonging Heiberg's description of Kierkegaard's religious development, which stopped at the 19th June 1852, to February 1853, where he demonstrates a fresh and higher awakening. Referring to the note (June 19, 1852) in which Kierkegaard expresses his resolve to go on spending his capital and moreover declares himself happy and confident, Geismar says: "Heiberg interprets this to mean that through this last sacrifice Kierkegaard has entirely broken down the wall that separated him from God and thus also conquered his melancholy, so that with this a healing process for "the thorn in the flesh" has come to an end; nor have we felt anything of it except in connection with the attempt to preach, and there Kierkegaard expressly says that he has not felt it for a long time.—To the very last P. A. Heiberg regarded the onslaught on the Church as the intrinsic factor in Kierkegaard's life.

And he quite realises that in his conception of the crisis and its cure this subjective view plays a part. His opinion of the Church polemics he has stated so definitely to me that it grieves me that he is no longer among the living so that he could protest against my asserting another view and possibly profaning Kierkegaard's memory by taking the edge off the point that had been sharpened by such enormous sufferings. It grieves me. For I myself feel that I have an immense responsibility if I wrongly say something that dulls the point. Nevertheless I must add that I cannot regard June 1852 as a complete cure. In reality something else happened. His melancholy was pervaded by reflection to such an extent that it no longer appears as something independent beside it; it has become fused with it; it has forced him mainly to select that which hurts out of the whole fullness of Christianity, and only to include mercy in so far as it was necessary to prevent disruption" (IV, pp. 125-26).—So he points out another awakening in February 1853, which is said to result in Kierkegaard cancelling what he had established in 1852. A fragment of the most important of the entries which Geismar uses for the documentation of his contention reads as follows: "Without standing in an immediate relation to God I have thought it right that I should take over the suffering which corresponds to standing in an immediate relation to God. The apostle, the disciple in that sense, stands in an immediate relation to God, and in that is the strength to endure sufferings which are superhuman, and in that also the exemption from using one's intelligence. A human being has only a mediate relation to God, and, being responsible to God, has to use his intelligence, and is responsible too if he does not use it— — —. On the other hand, I have felt in accordance with God, in delaying as long as I have a competency, in awaiting what is God's pleasure with me" (IV, pp. 128-29).—It is not seen that these statements revise, and do not on the contrary repeat, Kierkegaard's resolve and self-understanding from June 1852. He intends to keep things going with his capital but not to force himself into the sufferings of martyrdom, to which only the apostles and disciples, i.e. those who stand in an immediate relation to God, have access, that is to say: "Mercy is the decisive thing, but the imitation must be taken up; however, neither I nor others are alarmed beyond capacity, therefore I am only a poet— — —" (Heiberg: Rel. Udv. 374).

In the antagonism on this point between Heiberg and Bohlin, Geismar as in numerous other cases, sides with the latter when he needs must, but tries to save as much as possible of Kierkegaard's person and works for the sound Church life and Christian life. The enduring impression of the work therefore is its more personally motivated than methodically supported attempt to reconcile and smooth out.

BOHLIN's book "Søren Kierkegaard, the Man and his Work" (1939) has essentially the same disposition as Geismar's six-volume work; first Kierkegaard's history is carried up to 1841, after which the philosophy of the stages is systematically reviewed. Then the biography is continued up to the Corsair feud, and is followed by an exposition of the basic thoughts of the Christian production 1846-52. Finally Kierkegaard's inner debate and his outer life in his last years are described, and this forms the transition to the final acount of the onslaught on the Church.

The argumentative parts of Bohlin's book are in all essentials a brief and clear summary of the contents of his two larger books. He explains and teaches in a systematic form, quotes sparingly, and only exceptionally reports. The problems that are solved and the lines followed in these chapters are therefore precisely those which can be viewed from the standpoint Bohlin has chosen and which we have discussed above.—In the biographical sections of the book Bohlin has incorporated the results of the greatly increased biographical literature after Geismar's time. Bohlin does not lose himself in details and, probably on purpose, refrains from repeating the more fanciful discoveries, but his survey of the main events testifies both directly and indirectly to confidence in both Heiberg's, Brandt's, and Helweg's studies on the whole.

Of late years Bohlin's sober and compactly written book has become the one recommended to an academic reader as an introduction to Søren Kierkegaard: it is also firm and authoritative as a textbook. But no one would guess from it, if it were not also mentioned there, that Kierkegaard's production today is a living and active spiritual force. Here Kierkegaard is put in order, the greater part of the problems are solved, and of his thought the tares have been sorted from the wheat. The perspective may be deep, but never any deeper but that an academic theologian of Lutheran observance may grasp it.

So far the last general view is given in JOHANNES HOHLENBERG's (b. 1881, writer) two books "Søren Kierkegaard" (1940) and "Den Ensommes Vej" (The Way of the Solitary, 1948). The two books may be read independently of each other but are meant to be a connected work. The disposition, however, was given at the outset, the first part being written with a view to a publishers' competition about the best Danish biography. The book gained the prize and thus obtained a wide circulation. The first part describes the man, the second part the work. But Hohlenberg can hardly have had any objection to this arrangement of the material, for in contrast with the majority of Scandinavian students of Kierkegaard, he does not regard Kierkegaard's external fate as the basis of his production or his private conflicts as the causes of his spiritual changes of course. The intellect, the genius, is regarded as the primary factor which has formed both his history and his work, and the biography and the production can therefore be presented separately as different aspects of the same mental development.

Now Hohlenberg combines this theory with a view of life of a rather unusual kind; we shall say no more about it than is strictly necessary. The gist of it, as far as can be seen, is that the single subject is an "autonomous existence and microcosmic unit", which through a continued existence in various incarnations strives, or should strive, after an ever higher evolution and in this way raise the world to an ever more comprehensive consciousness and thus complete the unfinished work of creation. It might be expected that this theory which makes Hohlenberg entirely opposed to all continuations of the typical cultural life of the 19th century, political democracy, experimental and applied natural science, the attempts to introduce positivistic methods in the liberal sciences, must also make him hostile to and suspicious of the personal historical researches based on the assumption of a causal connection in the psychic domain, too. But Hohlenberg includes all the good stories, even the trumpet with which Poul Møller is said to have awakened the young Kierkegaard. For though he denies the belief in the decisive influence of external causes on the individual mind, i.e. the significance of biological inheritance, environment, financial independence, etc. so that there is reason to fear that a very meagre biography will be the result, nevertheless all external circumstances and happenings regain their validity by the fact that the genius must be supposed to have chosen its circumstances in a prenatal existence from the point of view as to whether they would favour and support its effect. Søren Kierkegaard's history will then not become dramatic in a trivial sense, but in a literal sense, will be a prearranged fate which will seem determined by external circumstances to naive spectators only. But to the reader it is of no decisive importance in the long run whether it is said that Kierkegaard was born as the child of such and such parents, or that he chose a particular, suitable married couple for his parents and let himself be born; it will be a matter of habit or might be so; indeed, for convenience Hohlenberg does not keep to this form of language either, for instance he does not write that Kierkegaard selected a manic-depressive psychosis, but that he suffered from it.

The biography is therefore lively; Heiberg's "Episode", Brandt's "The Young Søren Kierkegaard", and numerous imperfectly transmitted anecdotes are incorporated in it unabridged. Only the sympathy is unreservedly on Kierkegaard's side. It is, if not the biography of a saint, at least that of a hero. Kierkegaard's enemies are Hohlenberg's enemies; his unverifiable, but improbable, stories about molestation from the mob are regarded as history, and his immense private expenditure is wholeheartedly defended. It is a well-written, entertaining book, but not very critical with regard to the sources.

Hohlenberg himself considers his last book more weighty than the biography and so foresees that it will have a harder fate. In the preface to the second book he speaks with astonishing contempt of the literature he had availed himself of for the first one. But it is right that "The Way of the Solitary" is a better and more independent work, and it is the first of its kind. The five-sixths of the book (i.e. about 250 pages) consist in an explanatory survey of Kierkegaard's total production. The works are arranged in main groups according to the kind of author's name printed on their title pages, that is to say: the pseudonymous writings, Climacus and Anti-Climacus, anonymous writings, writings in his own name. The chapters are preceded by one called "The pseudonymous Authors", in which Kierkegaard's (varying) plans with his pseudonymity are elucidated, and in which a fanciful description is given of what the different authors must be supposed to have looked like, how they dressed, earned their living etc., a valuable and original chapter. But the main contribution despite all is the excellent analysis of the individual works; here the presentation of the problems in the numerous books is reproduced vividly and flexibly, the complicated Kierkegaardian formulation is simplified, but the intellectual milieu and thought construction are preserved. It is done with skill, nor could it have been done without.—In the last, undiscussed, part of the book Hohlenberg gives his estimate of Søren Kierkegaard's work on the basis of his personal conviction, and it must be supposed that the majority of readers will take no interest in these chapters. But by virtue of its main part this book, I think, must in spite of all be regarded as the best introduction to Søren Kierkegard's production with all its problems. It does not solve the Kierkegaardian problem, but it uncovers many of the strands and knots in the ingenious texture of his authorship and promotes and facilitates the reader's personal absorption in the works.

INDEX